Aggregation and
Disaggregation
in Sociology

Aggregation and Disaggregation in Sociology

Michael T. Hannan
Stanford University

Lexington Books
D. C. Heath and Company
Lexington, Massachusetts
Toronto   London

Published simultaneously in Canada.

Printed in the United States of America.

International Standard Book Number: 0-669-74393-3

Library of Congress Catalog Card Number: 76-156143

To my parents

Table of Contents

List of Figures and Tables

Preface

The pace of methodological innovation and advance in sociology seems to have markedly quickened in recent years. An important component of this advance involves application of the methods of linear causal analysis developed in econometrics and biometrics to problems arising in sociological research and theory construction. An examination of recent literature suggests that these developments have begun to have an impact on empirical research in the discipline. Examples of applications of Simon–Blalock techniques and path models are beginning to appear in a wide variety of substantive areas. This trend offers potential for real advance and at the same time poses significant challenges both to methodologists and to researchers. Much of the potential for advance lies in improved possibilities of replication and cumulation of nonexperimental research. Such possibilities are enhanced by the requirement that many of the assumptions underlying the construction of a model and the gathering and analysis of data be made explicit.

The restrictiveness of the assumptions underlying these regression-based techniques also gives rise to the challenges alluded to above. Given the state of both theory and data in the nonexperimental social sciences, it is highly unlikely that all of the assumptions underlying any one of the techniques will be met in any substantively interesting application. In other words, complications are almost certain to arise when substantive specialists employ techniques of linear causal analysis. As the techniques are applied to an increasing variety of empirical situations, the complications are likely to become quite diverse. Advocacy of the use of linear causal techniques demands an examination of the impact on inferences of those complications which are thought to be most probable in specific substantive areas. A number of the econometricians and biometricians who have pioneered in the development of the techniques under discussion have devoted considerable attention to complications. Among those which have received the most attention are errors in variables (including measurement error), errors of specification, multicollinearity, identification problems, autocorrelation, the introduction of unmeasured variables, and changes in units of analysis.

Undoubtedly, as sociologists continue to employ techniques of linear causal analysis they will encounter many of the same complications found in economic or genetic applications. In such cases, we should be quick to borrow established problem formulations and solutions if any exist. At the same time, given the differences in theoretical perspective and problem definition, it would be surprising if sociologists did not encounter some complications that are as yet unanalyzed. I would suspect that the most usual case would be the one in which the complications facing the sociological researcher are analogous to those faced in other disciplines but contain a component specific or unique to sociological investigations. A sophisticated use of linear causal analysis strategies requires a considerable amount of research into potential complications.

This analysis is concerned with one type of potential complication: *the effects of changes in levels of aggregation on parameter estimates in linear causal analysis.* This includes changes in levels in a single research design, e.g., when data gathered on one level are used to make inferences for another level, as well as comparing results of researchers working at different levels. Included in the scope of this analysis are changes from lower to higher levels (aggregation), as well as changes in the opposite direction (disaggregation). Much of the first chapter will be devoted to specifying the problem in some detail. But, broadly speaking, I am addressing myself to the well-documented effects of changing levels on the results of statistical estimation procedures (and, by extension, on the results of regression-based linear causal analysis techniques). I have attempted to survey analyses and explanations of such effects in a number of disciplines (principally sociology, econometrics and mathematical economics, political science, applied statistics, and statistical geography) in an attempt to explicate such effects in an abstract and general way.

Most of the best analyses of aggregation problems available have been done by economists writing at a level of mathematical sophistication beyond the training of most sociologists. I had originally intended to survey analyses in a number of fields and organize them in terms of these powerful and abstract formulations of the aggregation problem. This aim quickly raised questions concerning the appropriate audience for this endeavor. As I attempted to present the mathematical results in such a way that they might be relevant to nonmethodologists, I found that the larger issues tended to become submerged in the minutiae of technical arguments. Since Green [1964] has already systematized this body of results for economists, I decided that those who wish to pursue the mathematical argument would be better served by consulting his monograph and the papers cited therein. Thus, I have attempted to minimize here the mathematical complexity of this presentation to the point that a reading of this report should demand no more of the reader than competence in elementary applied statistics and familiarity with the basic strategies and techniques of causal modeling (as presented, for instance, by Blalock [1964]). Chapter 2 is an exception, in that it requires familiarity with elementary calculus (reviewed in Appendix A).

In attempts at making the mathematical treatments meaningful to the nonmethodologist, one perspective on the problem of changing units which did not at the outset play a central role became increasingly useful. I found over and over again that an explicit causal perspective along with use of the more familiar calculus of linear causal analysis was very helpful in attempting to bring abstract theorems to bear on practical research problems. More important, I began to find that such a perspective is extremely useful in specifying the relevance of mathematical analyses for empirical research. Thus, I have now come to the position of relating a wide variety of results on aggregation and disaggregation to the concerns of the causal modeler. The further I have gone in this, the more I appreciated the value of Blalock's [1964, ch. 4] formulation of the problem of changing units. The present analysis is in large measure a continuation and elaboration of that earlier effort.

A preliminary version of this work appeared in the Methodology Working Papers series of the Institute for Research in the Social Sciences at the University of North Carolina [Hannan 1970a].

M.T.H.
Stanford, California
June 1971

Acknowledgments

A considerable number of sociologists have contributed to this book in one way or another. I cannot mention all who made helpful comments in seminars and colloquia. However, I would particularly like to acknowledge the thoughtful comments of Israel Adler and John W. Meyer on earlier drafts. I also received helpful comments from K. Namboodiri, James Wiggins, Lewis F. Carter, and Charles Bowerman.

I owe an enormous debt to Hubert M. Blalock under whom this work was conceived and begun. His intellectual stimulation and encouragement greatly aided the work reported here.

The Laboratory for Social Research at Stanford University provided assistance in the preparation of this manuscript. Alison Wilson, Judy Liggett, and Anne Sklensky provided extremely competent typing labors.

**Aggregation and
Disaggregation
in Sociology**

1 Approaches to Changing Units of Analysis

There are a number of points of view from which the sociologist can approach the general issues concerning changing units of analysis in empirical research. Blalock noted in this respect:

One of the most challenging problems that continually arise in almost all substantive fields within the social sciences is that of just how one translates back and forth between the macro level, where groups are the unit of analysis, and the micro level where the focus is on individuals. The problems are both conceptual and empirical: there are questions of definition, aggregation, and the practical limitations of time–cost factors in gathering data on both levels. [Blalock 1967, p. 21].

To begin at the most abstract level, it is a far from simple matter to separate those issues which are empirical (the focus here) from those that are conceptual or theoretical. It is becoming increasingly apparent that this distinction between theoretical and methodological concerns is both artificial and limiting from the perspective of advance in either area. Theoretical formulations have important consequences bearing on the appropriateness of research designs, and estimation and testing procedures. Similarly, methodological strategies often constitute implicit theoretical positions.

Thus, while our concerns are methodological, we cannot completely avoid the theoretical (or, perhaps, metatheoretical) issues involved. In particular, we wish to make several points concerning major theoretical positions on the issues involved. This is necessary principally because the import or relevance of the abstract results to be developed in the chapters that follow is to a great extent dependent on the reader's metatheoretical assumptions.

Major Metatheoretical Positions on Changing Units of Analysis

Wagner has produced a very useful typing of theoretical "schools" in terms of positions on the issue of changing units. He notes:

Nineteenth century sociology, as a new type of social philosophy with scientific ambitions, penetrated the ranks of the older "social sciences" on a macrocosmic

1

scale. Microsociology, by contrast, is a product of the early twentieth century. . . . With its appearance, that particular dualism of scope with which we are concerned here was introduced into our discipline. . . . Yet, it is characteristic for the discontinuity of our discipline that even the mere existence of the problem has been recognized only sporadically . . . the differentiation of scope poses serious problems of theoretical consistency as well as general coherence of the discipline. Among these problems, that of the transition from micro- to macrosociological considerations and expositions is crucial. [Wagner 1964, p. 572]

Wagner was particularly concerned with the "fallacy of displaced scope" which occurs "whenever a theorist assumes, without further ado, that theoretical schemes worked out on the basis of macrosociological considerations fit microsociological interpretations, and vice versa" [Wagner 1964, p. 583]. Such tendencies are clear in at least two contemporary sociological "schools":

Structure-functionalism starts with the conception of social system and sees smaller units, down to the individual, as structural subparts whose functions are essentially defined and confined by the whole system. Interpretive-interactional theories, by contrast, start with the individual actor and view larger wholes as results of the interlinkages and interrelations among a multiplicity of individual actors. . . . Thus exponents of both approaches do not consider themselves limited to a certain scope of the sociological subject matter. In fact, most of them claim that their theory is applicable to the whole range of the micro-macrosociological continuum. [Wagner 1964, pp. 577–578]

Clearly, the translation of theoretical relations across levels of social organization is "fallacious" only given certain metatheoretical presuppositions. What is crucial from our perspective is not that two major approaches to theorizing have a tendency to displace scope (to use Wagner's terminology), but that these positions either implicitly or explicitly posit a basic *consistency* across levels of analysis. Wagner labels this the *homology thesis*. A particularly straightforward example of this tendency in modern sociological theorizing is presented by Talcott Parsons:

. . . the contrast between small scale partial social systems and the large scale is not on the same order as the shift from personality or psychological to social system or from organism to psychological. . . . There are continuities all the way from two person interaction to the United States as a social system. . . . That is why I emphasize the *theoretical continuity*, for the primary group offers powerful research tools. If this theoretical continuity is genuine then you can generalize from levels where things are demonstrated most freely, to other levels. [Parsons 1956, pp. 190, 194]

Parsons, of course, is by no means alone in this belief. In general, it appears that theorists who, like Parsons, engage in general-systems approaches find this assumption (homology across levels) a useful one.[1] Similarly, to the extent that formulations inspired by Marxian or neo-Marxian models assume that the behaviors of individual actors are reflections of structural arrangements, they also (implicitly) posit the homology thesis. This, then, is one polar position on the issue of changing units at the theoretical level.

There are, however, many points of view which reject the model of simple continuity. This is generally true of neoevolutionary, ecological, and demographic approaches. Such a *discontinuity thesis* is adopted not only by macrolevel theorists but also by microtheorists such as Blau and Homans. Homans has treated this issue explicitly:

In their private speculations, some sociologists were once inclined to think of the small informal group as a microcosm of society at large: they felt that the same phenomena appeared in the former as in the latter but on a vastly reduced scale—a scale that incidentally made detailed observation possible. And no doubt there are striking resemblances between the two. . . . But to say that the two phenomena have points in common is not to say that one is a microcosm of the other, that the one is simply the other writ small. . . . The reason lies . . . in the fact that, in the institutions of society at large, the relations between the fundamental processes are more complex. [Homans 1961, pp. 379–380]

This is an obvious polar alternative of the first position discussed.

We have greatly oversimplified complex issues in sociological theory and theory construction to make this important distinction. It is not surprising to find such marked disagreement among present-day theorists on the question of homology. It seems unlikely that there are any clearly superior strategies here. Whether or not an analyst profits in positing homology across levels of social organization depends largely on at least his substantive concerns, and the state of development of the theory. While our own position is largely a discontinuity one, we can remain agnostic on the issue for the present methodological investigation. The point of this discussion is that the interpretation of our results depends on the position taken by a given researcher (or the implicit position built into the theory he is testing) on the homology question. Those who operate from discontinuity perspectives will certainly expect to find large and important differences in analogous models estimated at different levels of aggregation. However, to those who operate from continuity or homology assumptions, such effects should be quite disturbing. Since these effects would not have any direct theoretical meaning, the variations in estimates obtained at different levels must be considered a "statistical artifact."

---

[1] Sprout and Sprout [1965] offer a criticism, on similar grounds, to the use of general-systems approaches in political science.

The development of interest in the "aggregation problem" in economics is an interesting example of the second type of reaction. While not all classic theory in economics is microtheory[2] (formulated in terms of "elementary" decision-making units), the prevailing direction of theoretical movement has been from well-developed microtheory to macrotheory (where relations among properties of entire economic systems is the focus). Thus, the microtheories have temporal priority; and most economists accord micromodels ontological priority as well. (It is commonly argued that a causal understanding of economic systems can be arrived at *only* with reference to economic decision makers.) Among the early attempts at quantitative macromodel construction was Tingbergen's [1939] work in which macrorelations were assumed to be the *averages* of corresponding microrelations. Such attempts immediately raised the question of consistency between predictions from microtheory and from this synthetic type of macrotheory. The work of Keynes [1936] raised additional questions. Here, there was no direct linkage of macro- and micro-theory. Instead, the theory was formulated in terms of the relations of sectors of the economy and aggregates of sectors. This strategy produced a debate among econometricians over the conditions under which this procedure would give rise to empirical specifications which would be consistent with those arrived at by microtheory.[3] This debate produced important analytic results which are reported in the next chapter.

The point here is that many economists expected to find consistency between analogous micro- and macromodels. When it became clear that one typically obtains inconsistent predictions from the two, reference was made to "aggregation bias." As we noted above, such inconsistencies must be thought of as bias in the context of a homology metatheory.

The theoretical perspectives involved in economic analyses seem to have shifted somewhat with the current emphasis on "general equilibrium theory" which provides alternative ways of conceptualizing aggregation problems.[4] While this development is not directly relevant to our concerns, it points to an issue not yet raised. The ideal solution (from a continuity perspective) to change-of-levels problems would be the specification of "auxiliary theories" connecting micro- and macroprocesses. General equilibrium theory is assumed to serve this purpose for a number of economic concerns. Sociologists and political scientists have recently become quite explicit about the need for "linkages" between micro- and macromodels.[5] More abstractly the

---

[2] See Peston [1959].

[3] See Klein [1946], Pu [1946], May [1946], and Nataf [1948].

[4] See Quirk and Saposnik [1968].

[5] See, for example, Price [1966].

problem can be seen as revolving around the absence of adequate "composition laws."

The aggregation problems we address involve only primitive kinds of compositions. We allow the grouping of microobservations into macro-observations. But the composition laws we ultimately need must involve the groupings of *relations* in systematic ways. Sociologists have made tentative efforts to address the composition-law problems (see the discussion of "structural effects" models in Chapter 6) but little theoretical work has been reported. The absence of adequate composition laws becomes very salient in the methodological analysis reported here. We will continually emphasize the need for what we call "cross-level auxiliary theories" for the resolution of a variety of methodological problems. Thus, while the focus of this book is methodological rather than theoretical (in the usually accepted sense of the term), the analysis leads insistently to the conclusion that methodological roadblocks will be satisfactorily resolved only by theoretical advance. More precisely, we need theories which specify relationships across levels of social organization. Hopefully, abstract methodological analysis will suggest critical problems for such theoretical work.

Methodological Positions

Methodologists have concerned themselves with the operational specification of cross-unit designs. That is, they have focused primarily on the possibilities of making inferences from results at one level to other levels. They have adopted discontinuity perspectives with seeming unanimity. Galtung, for example, argues:

The "fallacy of the wrong level" consists not in making *inferences* from one level of analysis to another, but in making direct *translation of properties or relations* from one level to another, i.e., making too simple inferences. The fallacy can be committed working downwards, by projecting from groups or categories to individuals, or upwards, by projecting from individuals to higher units. [Galtung 1967, p. 45]

Attention of the discipline was focused first on problems of disaggregation in W. S. Robinson's [1950] well-known paper. He demonstrated that measures of correlation for propositions can vary widely at different levels of aggregation and thus that it is incorrect to make inferences from results on aggregate data to the individual level. His position has become firmly entrenched as a methodological canon. Scheuch [1969, p. 138] notes that, "The ecological fallacy (or group fallacy) has come under sufficient scrutiny that we can now consider most of the problems raised as intellectually settled, even though in practical research these errors continue nearly unabated."

Galtung has defined this "fallacy" broadly enough to include movement to levels of analysis *below* the individual level:

Corresponding to the ecological fallacy one level above we would have this kind of fallacy:
A correlation is found between two variables applying to individuals. For analytical purposes the individual is seen as a boundary for subunits, such as psychological syndromes, role-behavior and status-behavior, time-slices in behavioral sequences, etc. The ecological fallacy in general consists in this: *properties found to be correlated at the higher level are assumed correlated, i.e., found within the same unit, at the lower level.* Here the fallacy would consist in believing that, because two behavioral elements are found within the same individual, they are also found in the same behavioral, temporal, spatial or mental contexts, we may choose to subdivide the individual into. And vice versa: if correlations are not found for individuals, could it not be that they still hold for the subunits. [Galtung 1967, p. 46]

Although this is a potentially useful formulation, for purposes of simplicity we will consider individuals as the most "primitive" units for the remainder of the analysis.

Until recently, the problems involved in changing units upwards were not so generally recognized. However, Riley [1963] suggested that there is an *atomistic fallacy* analogous to the ecological fallacy. Similarly, Scheuch [1965] directed attention to an *individualistic fallacy*. Coleman [1964] addressed himself to the issue of using simple aggregate measures as substitutes for structural measures. He argues that the simplifying assumptions (of homology) underlying such procedures ignore the central tenet of sociology, that social behavior is patterned. While such assumptions are suitable for investigating the invariant and simple homogeneous structure of molecules in a thermodynamic system, say, they are not, according to Coleman, suitable for the study of social behavior.

Now, if individuals in groups behaved this way, so that no structure of relations involved in other than random interactions, then they too could be considered an "aggregate body" for the purpose of group level concepts and laws. . . . But, ... In short, the very essence of society is a nonrandom structure of some sort. [Coleman 1964, p. 88]

Referring to the use of simple sums (and by extension, means and proportions) as structural measures, Coleman argues that unless the addition operation corresponds to some social phenomenon, the group level concept has no meaning other than as a kind of "aggregate psychological concept."

This is a rather rigorous statement of the discontinuity thesis at the operational level.

Common Implicit Positions

Assumptions adopted for the sake of convenience, such as those legitimating the use of parametric statistical procedures, often constitute implicit substantive presuppositions. This appears to be true with respect to the homology thesis, i.e., there are approaches to research and theory testing which place the analyst in the position of implicitly subscribing to the homology thesis at the level of his operationalizations. In particular, we would suggest that uncritical use of survey sampling procedures often implies consistency across levels of analysis. Coleman has commented on the individualistic bias which has characterized much survey research, particularly in the earlier stages of its popularity:

The individual remained the unit of analysis. No matter how complex the analysis, how numerous the correlations, the studies focused on individuals, as separate and independent units. The very techniques mirrored this well: samples were random, never including (except by accident) two persons who were friends; interviews were with one individual, as an atomistic entity. [Coleman 1958–1959, p. 29]

Galtung adds:

This individualism is further emphasized by building a probability model into the sampling procedure, so that the individual is torn out of his social context and made to appear in the sample as a society of one person to be compared with other societies of one person. In very heterogeneous societies like Mexico, Colombia, India such samples quickly lose any meaning. [Galtung 1967, p. 150]

This is not meant as a criticism of survey sampling or of sampling theory. The problem is uncritical use of sampling procedures, or perhaps secondary analysis of data collected for another purpose. The implicit assumption here inheres in choice of sampling frame.

There is another class of situations in which the homology thesis may be subscribed to at the operational level, which is perhaps more salient to present trends. These situations arise in attempts at constructing formal, particularly mathematical, models which are applicable at more than one level of analysis. Perhaps an example will help make this point. James Davis [1959] has attempted a formalization of relative deprivation theory which would integrate a range of empirical findings. His purpose, as is always the case in the construction of such models, was to proceed from a limited set of straight-forward axioms or assumptions which would enable him to use analytic techniques to derive consequences of the axioms (the remaining propositions of his theory). Indeed, the value of such formalizations is that they require that assumptions be made explicit and that they offer the possibility of deriving consequences of the model which might not be easily seen in a verbal representation of the same theory. The relative deprivation theory is suggested by the fact that in many interesting cases human groups or populations are partitioned (divided into two mutually exclusive and ex-haustive subgroups), on the basis of some criterion variable, into the deprived and nondeprived. The gratification of individuals is seen to depend not only on his objective conditions but also on the comparisons each makes with individuals who are similar to him on social variables but fall into the other subgroup on the criterion variable. Such comparisons are said to give rise to feelings of relative gratification or deprivation. Davis' contribution was to employ the calculus of finite probability theory to derive consequences of a simple model of this sort. However, to validate the use of probability theory, he was forced to make the following assumption: "Within the population, comparisons are random." [Davis 1959, p. 282]. In other words, it was necessary to assume that at least with respect to the phenomenon of interest there is no structuring of comparisons in human groups. Davis notes that this may appear implausible at the substantive level. Our interest is in what it asserts about the possibilities of consistency across levels of analysis. If comparisons are random as Davis is forced to assume, then there will be homology across levels.

Change-of-levels problems enter the testing or estimation of many mathematical formulations of social processes—indeed, even into Coleman's own work—in a less obvious manner. Most of the mathematical models which have been applied to social processes are formulated at the level of individual action, e.g., attitude change, occupational mobility, etc. Such models are specified in terms of individual propensities (probabilities of engaging in certain specified actions). However, such propensities cannot be estimated from the static empirical data usually available; and the use of time series observations will not completely sidestep aggregation problems since the analyst will likely face the need to aggregate over temporal observations for each individual. (See Chapter 5 for further discussion of temporal aggregation problems.) The most common solution to this problem is to employ aggregate relative frequencies to arrive at propensities for categories of individuals and then impute the same propensity to each individual in the category. Coleman, in presenting his basic continuous-time, discrete-space stochastic model notes:

This stochastic process is specified for an individual. In most cases, however, we will be dealing with aggregates of individuals, and except where otherwise indicated, we will assume that each individual is governed by the same transition rates. This means for n individuals there are n independent identical processes. [Coleman 1964, p. 108]

In another context, McFarland [1970] has identified the assumption involved as a *homogeneity assumption.* We will see in later chapters that change-of-levels problems do not produce serious mistakes in inference when such homogeneity assumptions are approximately satisfied. The point is, however, that *measurement models of the type just characterized result in disaggregation problems formally identical to those found when substantive propositions are disaggregated.*

We suspect that the issues raised in the chapters that follow will become increasingly obvious and problematic to sociologists as our theories become more formal and determinant and as more powerful estimation techniques are applied to their testing. For one thing, such developments will entail clearer specification of relations between variables and processes at different levels of analysis.

A Note on Fallacies

Much of the preceding discussion has been directed at labeling certain strategies and procedures as "fallacies." In the beginning stages of methodological investigation, preliminary statements tend to be stated in terms of the correctness or incorrectness of a procedure. It is common to label as "fallacies" those practices found to be lacking in rigor or logic. It is not wholly surprising that methodologists begin their investigations in this way. The history of theorizing in the social sciences demonstrates the prevalence of the tendency to begin theoretical formulations with dichotomies. And just as theoretical insight and advance is often achieved in the attempt to move from gross dichotomies and to specify dimensions of variables, metholodogical advance is often achieved in the attempt to move from a consideration of fallacies to analysis of error or bias introduced into inferences from research by certain procedures under specified conditions.

Absolute distinctions in sociological research methodology may be inappropriate and may tend to discourage research rather than improve its quality. It is this kind of reasoning which motivates statisticians to examine the robustness of elements (specifications) of a given statistical model or stochastic specification. The question is not whether a researcher is formally correct or not in using a given technique on some body of data, but rather, to what extent are his inferences likely to be distorted by specific biases. This is movement from either/or to variable thinking. Allardt has expressed a desire for such an approach to the analysis of the issues involved in changing units of analysis.

> The real issue in methodological discussions of today does not seem to be the ecological fallacy but rather the techniques used in analyzing data from many levels of social organization. . . . The discussion in terms of fallacies have tended to divert attention from asking questions about fruitfulness. [Allardt 1969, p. 45]

While we will not focus directly on fruitfulness, what follows deals with the magnitude of likely distortion introduced by changes in levels of analysis rather than with fallacies.

Further Relevance of the Problem of Changing Units

The current dominant opinion among sociologists appears to be that the issues raised by changing units of analysis in empirical research arise solely as a consequence of poorly conceived research designs. If this were the case, we might content ourselves with methodological caveats of the kind already cited. However, the problems of estimation and model construction discussed above present a potential difficulty which is not the consequence of poor technique; rather it derives from the kind of simplifications necessarily involved in many formalizations. We cannot easily dismiss the issue of changing units when formal models are involved.

Since the bulk of what follows is fairly abstract, it may be helpful to point to concrete analysis problems involving changes of levels which seem likely to confront many sociologists in ongoing work. We will mention four additional problematic situations.

Missing Data

In the quote with which we opened this chapter, Blalock noted that time–cost factors tend to prevent sociologists from gathering data at more than one level of organization. This presents a distinct potential problem for testing theoretical models directed at more than one level. Similarly it may be impossible or extremely costly to collect data on the level of analysis that most directly fits a specific research focus. Dogan and Rokkan point out that such difficulties are likely to occur in attempts at studying aspects of social structure as well as in individual level analyses:

There may be data for *individuals* across a range of areal units but no way of identifying the characteristics of the proximal community contexts of their behavior (for an ecological analysis). This is frequently the case in secondary analyses of nationwide sample surveys; for reasons of secrecy, or economy, or sloppy administration, there may no longer be any possibility of allocating individual respondents to any known set of primary sampling units.

The contrary situation is even more frequent: no individual data are at hand, but *aggregate* distributions have been established for territorial units at different levels. This is the case for a wide variety of official statistics: the primary individual data have either been kept secret from the outset, as in elections or referenda, or cannot be made available for administrative or economic reasons, as will often be the case for census data, school grades, tax records, criminal statistics. [Dogan and Rokkan 1969, pp. 5–6]

If the research problem is theoretically and substantively interesting, the researcher facing problems of missing data on the chosen level has no choice but to compromise his research design in an attempt to make inferences across levels.

Historical Analysis

The missing-data problems are likely to be particularly acute in historical studies where there is no possibility of collecting the appropriate data. Electoral analysts are presently able to overcome many of the difficulties posed for individual level analysts through use of opinion poll data and survey research. However, for past elections this is no longer a viable option. This problem is not unique to electoral analysis, but is likely to be faced in all studies of development.

An area of research in which ecological data are indispensible is *historical sociology and research* in general, insofar as it wants to include in its analysis the behavior of the anonymous masses rather than to limit itself to that of the elites who have left us personal documents. . . . To mention some specific data relevant for the political sociology of societies that made their transition to modernity in the nineteenth and early twentieth centuries, we have relevant data on voting, violence, strikes, political crimes, party and trade union membership, as well as data on the social structure from censuses, official social surveys, tax, educational, religious statistics, etc. [Linz 1969, p. 98].

The researcher desiring to test propositions formulated at the individual level will have no choice but to attempt some sort of disaggregation.

Comparative Research

There has been a tremendous upsurge of interest in comparative cross-national or cross-cultural research in recent years, stimulated by an interest in problems of socioeconomic development and modernization. Since 1962, the International Social Science Council has supported advance in the theory and methodology of such research. Major emphasis has been placed on "*quantitative* comparisons across different types of units and to the examination of alternative ways of improving the data bases for such comparisons" [Dogan and Rokkan 1969, p. 1]. Initially, this work featured data from *sample surveys* and *aggregate national statistics*.[6] This division of labor reflected the long-standing division in the social sciences between partisans of one or the other approach. However, shortly thereafter serious thought was given to attempting to combine approaches in comparative research.[7] This was at least partially stimulated by an awakened interest in comparative studies of within-nation variations. Comparative social scientists were not content to work at only two extreme levels of analysis: the individual and nation–state levels. One consequence of this interest was the planning of a "Symposium on Quantitative Ecological Analysis" at Evian, France in 1966.[8] One of the objectives of this symposium was "To review the possibilities of *joint strategies at several levels of aggregation*, particularly the possibilities of combining sample surveys of variations at the level of the individual with ecological analyses of the proximal contexts of such variations." [Dogan and Rakkin 1969, p. 12]. It would seem that an essential ingredient in such cross-level collaboration would be intensive methodological analysis of some of the issues already raised concerning effects of aggregation–disaggregation.

Data Archives

Closely related to the developments discussed above are the beginnings of several cross-national data archives. In such archives, empirical data originally

[6] See the reports in the special issue on "Data in Comparative Research," *International Social Science Journal* 16 (1964): 2–97; and Merritt and Rokkan [1966].

[7] See Rokkan [1965].

[8] The collection of papers edited by Dogan and Rokkan [1969] is in part a report of this symposium.

collected for a wide variety of purposes at various levels of aggregation will be codified and catalogued by topic area. Similarly, existing research results, often at varying levels of aggregation, will be classified and stored. Any attempt to utilize a series of such materials is likely to involve the researcher in issues relating to aggregation–disaggregation. The analyst may choose to aggregate or disaggregate available data, or may wish to separate the effects of level of analysis from other substantively interesting effects in comparing existing research results. In either case, efficient utilization of comparative data bank materials will often require additional attention to issues of changing units of analysis.

Summary

The thrust of the argument of this chapter is that levels-of-analysis problems arise in both theoretical and empirical activity and that the problems are not well understood in either area. This is not asserting the formal equivalence of conceptual levels-of-analysis problems with what we will be calling levels-of-aggregation problems. As we pointed out, aggregation problems may or may not result from an interest in shifting levels of analysis with theoretical statements. Sociologists seem to agree more on the nature of the methodological and empirical problems than about the theoretical problems. We argue, however, that the import of methodological arguments depends heavily on prior theoretical or metatheoretical assumptions.

More troublesome is the problem of formal inconsistency between theoretical and empirical assumptions built into much modeling activity and empirical research aimed at testing theoretical formulations. The main contention here is that such inconsistencies are inevitable (due to needs for simplification and the lack of appropriate data) and that a satisfactory methodology ought to deal with, among other things, the consequences for valid inference of various salient inconsistencies. This is an argument for the continued importance of problems arising from changes in levels of analysis and levels of aggregation. From this point, we will deal explicitly with the latter problem.

2 The Consistency Approach

The approach to levels-of-analysis problems presented in this chapter while abstract and general does not directly pertain to all types of aggregation–disaggregation problems. It is important, then, to clearly specify the properties of the aggreg...ion–disaggregation problems we will consider. We can do this by making two distinctions: macroprediction vs. microprediction and macrovariables which depend on microobservations vs. "global" variables.

Microprediction vs. Macroprediction

One common type of aggregation problem arises when the analyst is faced with a plethora of operationalized variables and for purposes of analytic and computational simplicity desires to reduce their number. Sociologists often think of such problems in terms of "data reduction." Consider the following highly simplified example of an occupational attainment prediction model:

$$y_i = f(x_{1i}, x_{2i}, x_{3i}, x_{4i}, x_{5i}, x_{6i}) \qquad i = 1, \ldots, N \qquad (2.1)$$

where

y_i is occupational attainment for the ith individual

x_{1i} is father's occupation

x_{2i} is father's income

x_{3i} is father's education

x_{4i} is IQ

x_{5i} is verbal ability

x_{6i} is ambition

For the reasons mentioned above the analyst may wish to reduce these variables to some lesser number by aggregating variables. For example, he might wish to define the following *composite variables:*

$$z_{1i} = f_1(x_{1i}, x_{2i}, x_{3i}) \quad \text{and} \quad z_{2i} = f_2(x_{4i}, x_{5i}) \qquad (2.2)$$

where z_{1i} is labeled "father's SES" and z_{2i} "general ability."

15

Given these definitions, it is possible to generate predicted values of the unaggregated dependent variable by means of two alternative empirical specifications. One prediction uses equation (2.1), the full micromodel. Call the array of predicted y_i values $\hat{y}$. The second prediction uses a composite function representation of the microrelation:

$$y_i = f(z_{1i}, z_{2i}, x_{6i}) \qquad i = 1, \ldots, N \qquad (2.3)$$

the abbreviated microrelation. Call this predicted array $\tilde{y}$. The issues of microprediction concern the agreement of the alternative predictions. One would like to make a reduction in complexity without losing a great deal of information or distorting the relationship of interest. Very concretely, the analyst desires that $\tilde{y} = \hat{y}$. Conditions under which this identity will hold are rather restrictive. Thus, methodological studies of microprediction issues tend to focus on conditions under which $\tilde{y}$ is a good approximation to $\hat{y}$. W. D. Fisher [1969] reviews a number of approaches to this general set of problems.

There is a subtle but important distinction between aggregating variables in a stochastic specification of a function relationship and aggregating the entire stochastic specification. Consider again the model for occupational attainment which is specified at the microlevel in equation (2.1). To demonstrate the second case, that of macroprediction, we allow each variable of (2.1) to be aggregated to a "corresponding" macrovariable by the following abstract *aggregation relations*:

$$y = y(y_1, \ldots, y_N)$$

$$x_r = x_r(x_{r1}, \ldots, x_{rN}) \qquad r = 1, \ldots, n \qquad (2.4)$$

Thus, for our seven-variable model we have seven aggregation relations which combine the $7N$ observations into seven observations. We can now postulate (usually by analogy) a relation holding among these seven variables which has the same functional form as equation (2.1). We call this the *macrorelation*:

$$y = F(x_1, \ldots, x_7) \qquad (2.5)$$

For example, if equation (2.1) holds at the individual level, equation (2.5) might be thought to hold for census-tract means. In this case, the aggregation relations are the operations which transform the responses of individuals to questions on the census survey into tract means.

Again, we see the possibility for two alternative methods of generating predicted values for the dependent variable (in this case the dependent macrovariable). Since the dependent macrovariable is functionally related to the array of dependent microvariable observations (by an aggregation relation), we can presumably predict the latter values by using the N micro-relations aggregating these predictions according to the aggregation relation defined in equations (2.4) to arrive at a macroprediction. Alternatively, one could operate directly on the single macrorelation. Issues of macroprediction concern the degree of agreement of generating predicted macrovalues. We return to this issue below. For the moment, the important distinction is that between aggregation of variables in relations and aggregation of entire empirically specified functional relationships. We concentrate solely on problems arising in the latter case. That is, we are concerned with the complications which arise when entire models are either aggregated or disaggregated.

Restrictions on the Macrovariables

In the previous section, we noted in passing that the analysis requires that micro- and macrovariables stand in some rather simple functional relation. The internal logic of the argument requires that we have a straightforward means of translating from the micromodel to the macromodel and back. The functional relations holding among sets of "corresponding" micro- and macrovariables provides this bridge.

We should note that this restriction excludes from the analysis models incorporating macrovariables which are by definition observed or inferred directly and which do not consist of operations on constituent units. Lazarsfeld and Menzel [1965] call such variables "global," and cite as examples the classification of societies on the basis of presence or absence of money as a medium of exchange or of "achievement motivation" in folk tales.

The functional relations holding between corresponding micro- and macrovariables we refer to as the aggregation relations. These relations not only specify which microobservations correspond with each macrovariable but express the rules according to which observations are grouped. In this sense, we will speak of the aggregation relations representing the *grouping criterion* (or criteria, as the case may be). Sociological interest has typically focused on those cases when microunits are aggregated into macrounits on the basis of location in some areal (administrative) unit. We call this *areal aggregation*. We show in the next chapter that aggregation of observations in a time series (*temporal* aggregation) is formally equivalent.

There is no logical necessity to limit our attention to areal and temporal aggregation. It is easy enough, however, to explain why interest typically has been restricted to these two types. We will see in the next chapter that the specification of aggregation effects or complications demands some ability to predict the effects of the particular grouping processes on the variation of the substantive variables. One must at least hazard a guess on this matter. Both areal and temporal aggregation share a common feature which simplifies the task of such prediction. Most analysts are willing, implicitly, at least, to assume that observations spaced closer in time or space are likely to be more alike on the average than observations spaced more distantly. We refer to this below as a "clustering" or "synchronization" effect which has something of the status of an empirical law. (See the discussion of spatial and temporal autocovariance in Chapter 3.) This is the key. Since analysts are willing to subscribe to this empirical generalization, they can make fairly precise specifications of the likely effects of various areal or temporal groupings on variation in their substantive variables.

If we are to extend this approach to more general cases, we must employ alternative empirical generalizations or propositions from substantive theories to the same end. Very often in sociological research, observations on microunits are grouped according to location in some formal organizational unit (e.g., class in school, cf. Hauser [1969] or location in some authority structure, cf. Aiken and Hage [1968]). In such cases, we must employ a knowledge of organizational processes to specify likely aggregation effects. For the sake of simplicity in what follows we will continue to refer to areal and temporal aggregation. But it is important to recognize possible extensions to more general cases.

An Abstract Formulation: the Consistency Criterion

To this point we have considered *microrelations* and corresponding *macrorelations*. The aggregation (and disaggregation) problems we are addressing arise in the comparison of parameter estimates associated with the mathematical representations (stochastic specifications) of the "same" model at different levels of aggregation. We can generalize about such problems only in the simplest of cases. As we just noted, the key assumption underlying existing analyses of the empirical effects of aggregation (and disaggregation) is that the micro- and macrovariables are functionally related. The rules which define macrovariables in this manner are referred to as *aggregation relations*. Thus, in any consideration of problems of aggregation we are concerned with the interrelations of three kinds of relations: microrelations, macrorelations, and aggregation relations. For a simple three-variable recursive model we can represent the situation as in Figure 2-1. Here X_1, X_2 and X_3

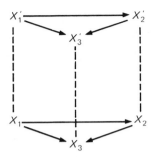

Figure 2-1. Analagous Micro and Macro Three Variable Causal Models.

are microvariables and X'_1, X'_2, and X'_3 are the respective corresponding macrovariables. We draw dashed lines from microvariables to corresponding macrovariables to represent the functional relations but for the present do not attach any causal significance to them. We can think of the other arrows as representing causal relations.

Aggregation issues generally arise when researchers begin with some well-established micromodel and form a macromodel by analogy to it. There are a number of clear examples in economics. Allen [1956] presents the following example. Consider a micromodel in which household demand for tea is a function of household income, the price of tea, and the price of several related commodities. One might posit by analogy that aggregate demand for tea is a function of aggregate income, the price of tea, and some general price index. It is in this sense of analogy that we are dealing with the "same" model at different levels of aggregation.

In studies embodying aggregation or disaggregation, as in much other research, sociologists have tended to employ dichotomous variables and to restrict themselves to pairwise comparisons. Economists are at a real advantage here since certain mathematical models are so embedded in economic theory that the coefficients of the models have direct economic meaning (e.g., marginal propensities to consume). We lack this easy translation from methodological issues to theoretically relevant models. The most obvious candidates for sociological examples are the cases which have given rise to the analyses of the issues raised by disaggregation: the study of the relationship of various social factors to suicide, crime, juvenile delinquency, mental illness, etc. It appears that these cases resulted in attempts at disaggregation because of the difficulty of obtaining individual level measures of "*propensities*" for suicide, etc. As a substitute for such individual measures.

researchers often shift levels and employ *rates* of certain behaviors. Selvin [1958] illustrates this tendency in Durkheim's *Suicide*. In an interesting comment on likely specification error in the study of the relationship of income level and suicide, Simon [1968, p. 302] noted in passing, "But as is common in work of this sort from here on we shall work only with somewhat vague pooled community analogies to the individual coefficients." Since such models are so often used in sociological analyses of the problem of changing units,[1] it might prove helpful to modify a model for predicting suicide rates from some of the variables identified by Durkheim. (The aim here is simplicity of statement for purposes of illustration; and no claim is made for the usefulness of this model—it is obviously oversimplified.)

Consider a model for predicting variations in suicide rates which takes such rates as a linear function of income level and several indicators of anomie: percent Protestant, percent of population of marriageable age unmarried and percent of married couples who are childless. This model does not address the individual-level questions of interest to many sociologists. (We will see the issues raised by attempts at disaggregation to estimates of individual level coefficients in Chapter 4.) It is possible that two researchers might seek to estimate the parameters of this model on different levels of aggregation using some regression-based procedure, say on the census-tract level and on the state level. The problem we are raising concerns the comparisons of the corresponding coefficients at the different levels. To employ the framework to be presented below, we would have to establish the aggregation relations by which census-tract totals or averages are transformed into state-level measures. It is difficult at this point to see the importance of considering the aggregation relations. This will become clear in the discussion presented in the next chapter.

Now that we have seen what the aggregation problem is likely to look like substantively, we can consider the issue of consistency. We have already noted that we must concern ourselves with the interrelations of three kinds of relationships. The analytic problem arises as a result of the functional dependence of macrovariables on corresponding microvalues. This functional dependence (expressed in the aggregation relations) results in more relationships than can be chosen independently, as inspection of Figure 2-1 would suggest.

Such a situation raises the possibility that the relationships may be defined in such a way as to be inconsistent with each other. Although the parallels are not completely clear, this situation seems analogous to the situation of overidentification of a model which allows the possibility that

---

[1] Cf. Boudon [1963].

the model may be inconsistent with certain sets of data. Here the possibility that the three key relations may be defined in ways which, when the three are taken together, give rise to inconsistencies, motivates the study of the conditions under which they will be consistent. Green for example, poses the problem as follows:

Consistency means that a knowledge of the "macro-relations" . . . and of the values of the aggregate independent variables would lead to the same value of the aggregate dependent variable as a knowledge of the micro-relations and the values of the individual independent variables. [Green 1964, p. 35]

Reference to our simple model will help clarify this concept. What does consistency require of the model drawn in Figure 2-1? The definition suggests that we are concerned with two different methods for generating predicted values of the dependent macrovariable. The first is the straightforward estimation of the macrofunction. We can denote the resulting predicted values $\hat{X}'_3$. The second procedure is an estimation of the microfunction for all microunits to obtain an array of predicted X_{3i} values and then to apply the aggregation relation to these predicted dependent microvariable values to generate a predicted macrovalue. We will denote this second predicted value $\hat{\hat{X}}'_3$. Following Green's definition, we will say that aggregation in this simple model is consistent if and only if $\hat{X}'_3 = \hat{\hat{X}}'_3$. If this equality does not hold, the difference $\hat{\hat{X}}'_3 - \hat{X}'_3$ is said to be due to the presence of *aggregation bias* in the parameters. It is the possibility of such aggregation bias in parameters which has stimulated most of the analyses of the aggregation problem.

We see that consistency has a very special meaning in the context of aggregation problems and should not be confused with the statistical concept of consistency. We should further note that since in consistent aggregation the estimate of the dependent macrovariable (e.g., state suicide rates) is the same for the two different methods for generating predicted values, *all* one gains in aggregation is efficiency in analyzing data for a large number of microunits. In other words, the consistency perspective rules out "emergent properties" in changes of levels of analysis. In this sense, the economists' notion of consistency can be considered a formalization of what we have called the homology thesis. A consistency approach implicitly rules out the possibility of significant substantive changes across levels.

We have emphasized that perhaps the majority of sociologists would reject the model of simple homology and would neither expect nor desire empirical consistency across levels of aggregation. Yet, the concept of consistency is useful because it can be formalized in such a way as to serve as a standard against which to judge the effects of changing units. It allows us to define aggregation bias in any particular case (conforming to the restrictions outlined above).

Two Broad Approaches

As Lancaster [1966] emphasizes, aggregation is not a single problem but presents a set of related problems. We have just commented on the lack of independence of the three relations involved in any case of (simple) aggregation. In a practical sense this dependence means that the analyst is free to specify only two of the relations. In other words, consistency requires (by definition) that once two of the relations have been specified, the third must have some restricted form. Much of the succeeding analysis can be seen as concerned with the necessary and sufficient conditions for the three relations to be consistent.

This freedom in specifying two of the relations has resulted in a concentration of effort (at least among economists and sociologists) on two broad approaches:

1. *Given a microtheory and microvariables, posit a macrotheory and then search for relationships between micro- and macrovariables consistent with the propositions on the two levels.* In the suicide rate example, this would involve a specification of the county-level suicide rate function and of the state-level suicide rate function and an attempt to define aggregation relations in such a way as to produce state-level variables which will result in consistent aggregation. In other words, this approach involves manipulating the definitions or operationalizations of the variables at different levels (i.e., manipulation of the aggregation relations) to achieve consistency. In economics, this approach has been advocated by Klein [1946] and has been developed exhaustively by Theil [1954, 1959].

2. *Given a microtheory and microvariables, define a set of macrovariables* (usually employing available aggregates, e.g., per capita income) *and search for a consistent macrotheory.* In the suicide-rate example, this would involve employing macrovariables such as per capita income, suicide rate per thousand population, etc., and then searching for a theoretically satisfying macrofunction which is consistent with the microtheory and the aggregation relations. This strategy has been advocated by May [1946].

Lancaster notes that the first strategy has been more widely used in empirical work where the focus has been on detecting the effects of using certain types of aggregates. The second strategy has been most appealing to microtheorists interested in extending their formulations to account for widely observed regularities among conventionally used aggregates.

It is somewhat awkward to fit our analysis into one or another of these approaches. The difficulty is that the aggregation–disaggregation problems faced by sociologists typically involve *no* unconstrained choice of relations. In almost all cases, the aggregation relations are constrained by the availability of data and the macrorelation is constrained by the requirement of homology with the microrelation or, in the disaggregation case, the microrelation is constrained by the requirement of homology with the macrorelation. The last point is quite important. We do not employ an inductive approach to the formulation of macrotheories but place theoretical constraints on the macropropositions we are willing to entertain. True, these constraints most often consist of analogies to better understood microrelations. However, we are not dealing here with issues of theory construction but with the methodological problems which arise when homology is posited (for one reason or another) across levels of aggregation.

Thus, our investigation parallels the first approach outlined above and we rely heavily on the approach taken by Theil. This perspective is very useful in precisely identifying the consequences of aggregation on inferences. We will eventually take issue, however, with the general strategy for resolving the consistency problem which emerges from Theil's approach. In sum, we are largely pragmatic in our choice of perspectives. We argue that the pursuit of the issues raised by Klein and Theil are more likely to lead to satisfactory formulations of our current methodological problems than is investigation of the issues posed by May.

The Fundamental Importance of Linearity

In this section, we present the major result underlying most analyses of aggregation problems. The result is a proof that linearity of all three relationships (micro-, macro-, and aggregation relations) is a necessary and sufficient condition for consistency even in the case of completely deterministic models. This is a very powerful result, which has quite general implications. Before taking up the argument, we should comment briefly on the literature we follow.

This analysis and much which follows in later chapters depends heavily on mathematical formulations of aggregation problems directed at economic applications. Any sociologist who intends to involve himself in the study of aggregation–disaggregation problems must, of course, work through the technical papers. Unfortunately, this is likely to be a frustrating experience for two reasons. First, the discussions typically assume considerable mathematical background. And, second, they tend to assume familiarity with rather specialized substantive models. The problem here is that there is often no clear distinction between assumptions made for the sake of the methodological argument and those made for the specific purpose of fitting the methodological argument to substantive concerns.

Despite these difficulties, it is essential that we utilize approaches which have proven useful in other disciplines. In particular, it is important that sociologists be made aware of the mathematical formulations relevant to aggregation–disaggregation problems. Our goal here is quite limited. Assuming familiarity with the calculus (review of essential points is presented in Appendix A), and following Green's [1964] organization, we will attempt to partially bridge the gap between the verbal statements of the aggregation problem and the mathematical proofs which underly major results. Emphasis, then, is on the structure of the argument and the motivation for the mathematical statement. Readers interested in more comprehensive treatment of the mathematical approaches available are referred to Green [1964].

We return to the problem of "data reduction" raised in the first part of this chapter. We noted there that in the interest of parsimony and systematic comparison we are continually forced to group observations in some way so as to reduce the number of entities under consideration. Economists often point to this need in the case of consumption functions. Given the enormous range of possible types of consumption behaviors, the theorist, no less than the researcher, must somehow group types of consumption which are "similar." Sociologists need only look to the "typological tradition" of the discipline to see the importance of such an activity. We are constantly faced with the need to group societies, organizations, delinquent or criminal acts, etc. in a manner which facilitates comparative analysis.

Of course, numerous approaches to the problem of data reduction are widely known in sociology, e.g., scaling models, factor analysis, cluster analysis, latent structure analysis. Unfortunately we lack a systematic framework which organizes all of the available data-reduction models. Here we consider one very useful abstract formulation of the data-reduction problem: an abstract statement for continuous functions of the conditions under which variables may be considered "similar" and thus may be grouped together without distortion. This approach concerns itself with the *functional separability* of variables and is due to Leontief [1947a, 1947b].

Leontief points out that establishing the conditions under which a known set of "subsidiary relationships" can be combined into one overall function such as equation (2.3) is trivial. The interesting and important question is under what conditions can we establish the consistency requirements which must be met by the subsidiary relationships working from a knowledge of the mathematical properties of the overall relationship. In other words,

Leontief was interested in deducing from the assumed properties of equation (2.1)—the overall relationship—the set of grouping procedures which would result in consistency as defined in equation (2.3).

Equation (2.3) defines for the example under consideration the "optimal" grouping procedure. But we need a more general statement of the conditions of functional separability under which grouping will be consistent as in (2.3). We begin with a more general overall or elementary function:

$$y = f(x_{11}, \ldots, x_{1n}, \ldots, x_{m1}, \ldots, x_{mn}) \tag{2.6}$$

Since notation is something of a problem here, we should be explicit. The notation in a sense "works backwards" from the composite function. We want to eventually be able to represent y as a function of only m variables. We define the elementary function on mn variables and the notation indicates that all x_{rk} will be grouped together as a composite variable x_r. That is, this notation makes it convenient for us to define a set of *grouping relations* as follows:

$$x_r = g_r(x_{r1}, \ldots, x_{rn}) \qquad r = 1, \ldots, m \tag{2.7}$$

Now that we have some grouping procedure we can define y as a function of the m composite variables.

$$y = F(x_1, \ldots, x_m) \tag{2.8}$$

We are interested in the restrictions which must be put on the grouping procedures in order that

$$y = f(x_{11}, \ldots, x_{1m}, \ldots, x_{m1}, \ldots, x_{mn}) = F(x_1, \ldots, x_m) \tag{2.9}$$

Leontief's strategy, then, was to consider the deductions we can make from our knowledge of the form of the elementary relation concerning the "permissible" groupings which would preserve the identity expressed in equation (2.9).

As we have already noted, we want to group variables which are "similar" with respect to the relationship involved. Obviously, the composite variables formed will be analytically useful only if all of the elementary variables included in each "behave alike" with respect to changes in other variables in the system. For continuous functions, the calculus provides us with a straightforward representation of this type of similarity, which we are calling functional separability. To see this we must consider a set of ratios of second-order cross-partial derivatives:

$$\frac{\partial f / \partial x_{rj}}{\partial f / dx_{rk}}$$

Expressions like this arise quite naturally in several applications of classical economic theory and are called "rates of marginal substitution." Consider a simplified version of the occupational attainment model presented earlier:

$$y = f(a, b)$$

where y is occupational attainment, a is father's occupation, and b is motivation. The total differential for this function is

$$dy = \frac{\partial y}{\partial a}\, da + \frac{\partial y}{\partial b}\, db$$

Consider the case

$$0 = \frac{\partial y}{\partial a}\, da + \frac{\partial y}{\partial b}\, db$$

This case is the approximate relation between increments da and db along a "constant occupational attainment curve." Since this relation holds for any point (a, b), we can define the following relation:

$$r = -\frac{db}{da} = \frac{\partial y/\partial a}{\partial a/\partial b}$$

The value r is the marginal rate of substitution of the factor A for the factor B in the determination of occupational attainment. This quantity represents the additional amount of motivation needed (from the combination of independent variables specified by the model) to maintain occupational attainment unchanged when a small unit reduction is made in father's occupation.[2]

We can state the requirements for functional separability in terms of the relationship of the rate of marginal substitution between factors in a grouping to other factors outside the grouping.

THEOREM 1. *Necessary and sufficient conditions for the equality in equation (2.9) to hold when the elementary variables x_{rk} are free to take on all non-negative values, are that for all q, r, i, j, k ($q, r = 1, \ldots, m$, $q \neq r$ and $i, j, k = 1, \ldots, n$)*

$$\frac{\partial}{\partial x_{qi}} \left(\frac{\partial f/\partial x_{rj}}{\partial f/\partial x_{rk}} \right) = 0 \tag{2.10}$$

or equivalently

$$\frac{\partial f/\partial x_{rj}}{\partial f/\partial x_{rk}} = \frac{\partial^2 f}{\partial x_{rk}\partial x_{rj}} (x_{r1}, \ldots, x_{rn}) \tag{2.11}$$

---

[2] This brief discussion is a modification of Allen [1936, pp. 240–245].

Equation (2.10) defines another quantity employed in classical economic theory, "the elasticity of the rate of marginal substitution." It indicates the change in the rate of marginal substitution as a function of changes in other variables in the system. The theorem states that a subset of independent variables is functionally separable if changes in the rate of marginal substitution of variables in the subset is *independent* of variables not in the subset. To continue the occupational attainment example, this would mean that father's income, education, and occupation form a separable subset of the function we defined if the marginal rates of substitution of these factors are independent of the individual's ability and motivation.

The second representation, equation (2.11), of the result of Theorem 1 simply states that the rate of marginal substitution between variables in a separable subset must be a function only of variables in that subset.

Through a series of further results which will not be presented here, the result on functional separability is extended to the aggregation of relations as we have previously defined this.[3] We will simply develop the formalization of aggregation of relationships and state the consequences for this problem of the extension of the separability result.

To this point in the discussion we have focused on a dependent variable at a single level of aggregation and have considered groupings of elementary independent variables. But, in our discussion of aggregation in the previous sections, we considered entire relationships at different levels of analysis. To develop a formalization of the aggregation problem we must shift our attention from a search for more efficient ways of predicting single dependent variables to the mathematical relations between the "same" substantive relationship at different levels of aggregation.

We now consider a set of *microrelationships*,

$$y_s = f_s(x_{1s}, \ldots, x_{rs}, \ldots, x_{ms}) \qquad s = 1, \ldots, n \qquad (2.12)$$

In terms of our example, we now have occupational attainment prediction equations for each of n individuals in some population. Note that we allow the possibility that each microunit has a distinct microfunction, and we will see that whether or not this is the case becomes quite important in analyzing the effects of aggregation. We now wish as before to establish a *macrorelation*,

$$y = F(x_1, \ldots, x_r, \ldots, x_m) \qquad (2.13)$$

---

[3] See Green [1964, Ch. 2].

where *both* the independent and dependent variables are aggregates, i.e., where there are *aggregation relations*,

$$y = y(y_1, \ldots, y_s, \ldots, y_n)$$
$$x_r = x_r(x_{r1}, \ldots, x_{rs}, \ldots, x_{rn}) \qquad r = 1, \ldots, m$$

(2.14)

The first result which is useful in analyzing aggregation problems (e.g., invalidating Theil's "perfect aggregation" method considered in Chapter 5) is the following:

THEOREM 2. *Necessary and sufficient conditions for the functions (2.12) to be aggregated to the function (2.13) when the microvariables are free to take on all values are that for all* $r = 1, \ldots, m$ *and* $s = 1, \ldots, n$

$$\frac{\partial F}{\partial x_r} \frac{\partial x_r}{\partial x_{rs}} = \frac{\partial y}{\partial y_s} \frac{\partial f_s}{\partial x_{rs}}$$

(2.15)

It is worthwhile to consider the simple proof of this theorem—which is little more than a restatement of the consistency criterion— since it presents an example of the type of deductions that can be made from the abstract consistency model. Recall that in developing the criterion of consistency we stated the requirement that predictions from changes in independent macrovariables to changes in dependent macrovariables along two different paths must be identical. We can use the rule for the total differential to restate the two paths abstractly:

$$dy = \sum_{r=1}^{m} \frac{\partial F}{\partial x_r} dx_r = \sum_{r=1}^{m} \sum_{s=1}^{n} \frac{\partial F}{\partial x_r} \frac{\partial x_r}{\partial x_{rs}} dx_{rs}$$

and

$$dy = \sum_{s=1}^{n} \frac{\partial y}{\partial y_s} dy_s = \sum_{r=1}^{m} \sum_{s=1}^{n} \frac{\partial y}{\partial y_s} \frac{\partial f_s}{\partial x_{rs}} dx_{rs}$$

Green's theorem simply establishes this equality as the criterion for consistent aggregation.

Finally, we come to the central result. Nataf [1948] employed extensions of the results on functional separability (which he developed independently of Leontief in a less general form) to demonstrate the crucial importance of linearity for consistent aggregation. His theorem (which is stated but not proven below) establishes that *consistent aggregation requires that all three relations, micro-, macro-, and aggregation relations, must be linear.*

THEOREM 3. *Necessary and sufficient conditions for the aggregation of the functions (2.12) to the function (2.13) when the microvariables* x_{rs} *are free to take on all nonnegative values (i.e., when we have no a priori information which* *allows us to set limits on the microvariables) are that there exist functions G, H, g_r, h_r, G_r, H_s, g_{rs}, and h_{rs} such that*

$$y = H[h_1(y_1) + \cdots + h_n(y_n)] = G[g_1(x_1) + \cdots + g_m(x_m)]$$

where

$$y_s = H_s[h_1(x_{1s}) + \cdots + h_{ms}(x_{ms})] \qquad s = 1, \ldots, n$$

and

$$x_r = G_r[g_{r1}(x_{r1}) + \cdots + g_{rn}(x_{rn})] \qquad r = 1, \ldots, m$$

The reader is urged to consult Green for an extended proof of this key theorem.

A simple application of these results is illuminating. Consider the case in which all macrovariables are simple *sums* of corresponding microvariables:

$$y = \sum_{s=1}^{n} y_s$$

$$x_r = \sum_{s=1}^{n} x_{rs} \qquad r = 1, \ldots, m$$

In this simple case, a unit change in one of the microvariables produces a unit change in the corresponding macrovariable, i.e., for all r, and s ($r = 1, \ldots, m$; $s = 1, \ldots, n$)

$$\frac{\partial y}{\partial y_s} = \frac{\partial x_r}{\partial x_{rs}} = 1$$

From Theorem 2 we see that necessary and sufficient conditions for consistent aggregation are reduced to the following: for all r, s, and t ($r = 1, \ldots, m$; $s, t = 1, \ldots, n$)

$$\frac{\partial F}{\partial x_r} = \frac{\partial f_s}{\partial x_{rs}} = \frac{\partial f_s}{\partial x_{rt}}$$

But $\partial F/\partial x_r$ depends only on the values of the sums $x_1, \ldots, x_m$. And, a given set of sums is consistent with an indefinite number of allocations of microvariables. In other words, given that there are some n microvariables contributing to each sum, it is possible that all of the contribution comes from any single microvariable, that the contribution is distributed uniformly across the set of microvariables, or any intermediate case. Knowledge of the sum does not contribute any information about the distribution. Thus, for the above identity to hold, the value of $\partial f/\partial x_{rs}$ must not only be equal for all s, but must be constant for all values of x_{rs}. It follows from this that the partial derivative of the microfunction with respect to a given microvariable must (for consistency) be equal to the partial derivative of the macrofunction with respect to the corresponding macrovariable. Since partial derivatives can be interpreted as partial slopes, it follows that the individual or elementary functions must be *linear with identical slopes.*

Consider the import of this result for our simplified occupational attainment model. This says that even if we operated in terms of exact linear micro- and macromodels and employed linear aggregation, specifically taking means of microobservations, we would not achieve consistent aggregation unless all of our microunits have identical occupational attainment prediction functions. In other words, all of the individuals in the sample we employ must be *homogeneous* with respect to the way in which they react to changes in our substantive independent variables in terms of occupational attainment. Here we see the extreme restrictiveness of the above result, and the reason that much of aggregation analysis focuses on the effects of heterogeneity on the aggregation and disaggregation of data. This concern will recur persistently in the chapters which follow.

There is one obvious case of nonlinearity that does not cause any particular difficulties. This is the case where the logarithm of the dependent microvariable is a function of the logarithms of the independent microvariables:

$$y_i = a_i x_{1i}^{b_{1i}} \ldots x_{mn}^{b_{mn}}$$

All of the conditions for consistent aggregation are met when one takes a logarithmic transform of this function and then aggregates terms. Note, however, that the macrovariables here have quite different substantive interpretation as they are not weighted sums but weighted products. Under *very* restrictive conditions, consistent aggregation may be achieved with some more general nonlinear functions. At the present time, sociological models are not well enough specified to make these developments salient.[4]

We should emphasize that *the theorems cited hold for deterministic as well as for stochastic models.* For the remainder of this analysis we will focus on the additional difficulties that arise when *linear* stochastic models are aggregated or disaggregated. All of what follows then presumes linearity of relations precisely because of the results just discussed.

Aggregation Bias as Specification Error

There is a very general way of considering aggregation–disaggregation problems as we have defined them which has not been mentioned yet. To

---

[4] Brief discussions of the restrictions involved are presented by Theil [1954, pp. 126–132] and Green [1964, pp. 42–44].

see this, let us briefly restate the problem as outlined in Chapter 1. We are dealing with the estimation and inference problems that arise when an empirical researcher employs a stochastic specification of a relationship which, from the point of view of his theoretical concerns, is at the incorrect level of aggregation. We have noted the case in which the analyst interested in a behavioral relation has access only to data on aggregates as well as the case of the analyst who must aggregate information from lower units in order to study some more macro processes.

This is a typical case of what is often called *specification error*:[5] Presume one has a microtheory which is correctly specified in terms of form of relationship, variables included, effects of variables excluded on those included, etc. However, let us assume that observations on behavioral units are not available but some aggregation quantities are. If one proceeds to employ these variables to produce estimates of the parameters of his micro-relation and to make inferences to his microtheory, he is using a misspecified model. This is a case of what is usually called "errors in variables." When the model calls for, say, individual income the analyst enters observations on community per capita income, etc. Obviously the specification error approach is extremely general and for this reason does not seem to suggest specific lines of inquiry into the effects on inferences of aggregation and disaggregation. However, it is useful to point out the formal analogy of aggregation–disaggregation problems with other persistent difficulties faced in quantitative methodology.

Having said this, it is important to distinguish aggregation–disaggregation problems from the most usual case of errors in variables, measurement error. From a theoretical perspective, the two problems have quite distinct features. To show this we refer back to the simple causal model presented in Figure 2-1. We alter this simple model in Figure 2-2 to include three new variables, X_1'', X_2'', and X_3''. These represent the "true" values of the macrovariables. Thus X_1', X_2', and X_3' are indicators (measured values) of the corresponding macrovariables. As before, the indicators are simple mathematical transformations of the microvariables. To avoid overcomplication we will assume that the microvariables are perfectly measured since this does not affect the argument.

The Durkheim suicide model fits this simple representation. The theoretical argument is stated in terms of "structural" or macroproperties which are assumed to be nonreducible to behavioral variables—the macrorelations. At the same time, hypotheses are stated in terms of individual behavioral units (e.g., unmarried persons, childless couples, etc.)—the microrelations. Finally,

---

[5] See Chapter 6 and the discussion by Theil et al. [1961, ch. 6].

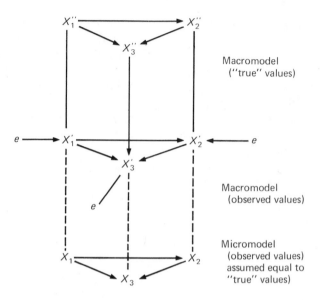

Figure 2-2. Figure 2.1 Revised: Aggregates As Indicators of Macro-variables.

aggregated individual properties or behaviors (rates, etc.)—the macro-indicators—are employed in the empirical tests.

We can use the model pictured in Figure 2-2 to point out the main difference between aggregation–disaggregation bias and measurement error. In any analysis of measurement error one is, by definition, considering the relationships between observables (measured values) and nonobservables (the "true" values), e.g., the relationship between X_1' and X_1''. We typically assume that the measured value is produced by the true value of the variable of interest; by a series of other factors summarized in a random disturbance; and, perhaps, by systematic biases. In the analysis of aggregation, the case of disaggregation error is quite different. In all cases, we consider relationships between observable quantities at different levels of aggregation. Further, we do not typically specify causal relations between corresponding variables at different levels of analysis, e.g., between X_1 and X_1'.

We should be careful not to overstate the case. Despite these important differences, both aggregation and disaggregation bias and measurement error are, as we originally pointed out, special cases of specification error. The goals of the analyst should determine whether or not it is useful to distinguish between the two. For our present concerns such a distinction is useful.

Summary

The scope of this analysis is limited to those cases of aggregation or disaggregation where entire stochastic specifications are aggregated or disaggregated. In such cases, a large number of relations are condensed into some smaller number (aggregation) or an attempt is made to recover the microrelations from some observed macrorelation (disaggregation). These cases must be distinguished from the aggregation problems that arise when variables are grouped for the purpose of economy of representation of a process at a single level of aggregation.

We formulate the aggregation–disaggregation problem in terms of the interrelations of three kinds of relations—microrelations, macrorelations, and aggregation relations—and study the conditions under which all three will be consistent. We see that inconsistencies in the definitions leads to aggregation (or disaggregation) bias even in deterministic models. The conditions for consistent aggregation are quite restrictive when no constraints (other than the requirement that macrovariables be related only to corresponding microvariables) are placed on the relationships involved. Necessary and sufficient conditions for consistent aggregation in this case are that all three relations be linear and when the macrovariables are defined as simple sums of microobservations consistent aggregation requires further micromodels with constant parameters.

3

Aggregation in Cross-Sectional Recursive Models

We begin the analysis of empirical aggregation effects with the simplest models employed by sociologists. In this chapter, we discuss the aggregation implications for cross-sectional recursive (or more generally single-equation) models. As we have already noted, sociologists have typically been more concerned with disaggregation problems. In fact, many of the results reported in this chapter first appeared in statements on disaggregation problems. Yet any analysis of the latter problem demands at least an implicit analysis of the logically prior problem of aggregation. That is, to understand the likely difficulties arising in the disaggregation of relationships, it is necessary to formulate some simplified model of what happens to data sets when they are aggregated in the "usual ways." The usual ways which have concerned sociologists are groupings according to residence in administrative areal units.

The reader will note that much of the following analysis is formulated in terms of bivariate relationships. This is typical of almost all sociological commentaries and analyses of the issues involved. After identifying the processes which can be seen to be creating aggregation complications in such limited models, we will address more complex models. We will see, however, that it quickly becomes very difficult to make precise statements about the aggregation complications arising in multivariate models. After considering the aggregation problem for static or cross-sectional models in some detail, we will return in the following chapter to the more traditional disaggregation concerns of the sociologist.

The Effect of Grouping on the Behavior of Correlation Coefficients

It has been known for quite some time that the correlation coefficient tends to inflate as the size of the units used is increased. Gehlke and Biehel [1934] presented an early example of this effect. They correlated male juvenile delinquency (expressed both in absolute terms and as rates) and median monthly rental for various groupings of census tracts in Cleveland. The 252 census tracts were successively grouped into larger and larger units on the basis of geographical proximity. The results are presented in Table 3–1.

35

Table 3–1. Relationship Between Delinquency Rate and Rental Value at Different Levels of Aggregation

Number of Units	Value of r (Absolute No. of Delinquents)	Value of r (Delinquency Rates)
252	−.502	−.516
200	−.569	−.504
175	−.580	−.480
150	−.606	−.475
125	−.662	−.563
100	−.667	−.524
50	−.685	−.579
25	−.763	−.621

Yule and Kendall [1950] present another example. They calculated the zero-order correlation between wheat yields and potato yields for 48 English counties to be .219. When they paired contiguous counties, the correlation rose to .296. When this process was repeated, the value of r became .576. When the resulting 12 units were grouped into 6 units, the correlation became .765. They addressed the obvious question of the meaning, if any, of these results:

On the face of it we seem able to produce any value of the correlation from 0 to 1 by choosing an appropriate size of area for which we measure the yields. Is there then, any "real" correlation between wheat and potato yields . . . ? [Yule and Kendall 1950, p. 311]

It might prove helpful to record the central statement of their position *verbatim* since the argument is not a clear one.

This example serves to bring out an important distinction between two different types of data to which correlation analysis may be applied. The difficulty does not arise when we are considering the relationship, say, between heights of fathers and sons. The ultimate unit in this case is the individual father or son whose height is a unique non-modifiable numerical measurement. We cannot divide a single pair of father-and-son into smaller units; nor can we amalgamate two pairs to give measurements of the same type as that of the single pair.

. . .

On the other hand, our geographical areas chosen for the calculation of crop yields are *modifiable* units, and necessarily so. Since it is impossible (or at any rate agriculturally impractical) to grow wheat and potatoes on the same piece of ground simultaneously we must, to give our investigation any meaning, consider an area containing both wheat and potatoes; and this area is modifiable at choice. A similar effect arises whenever we try to measure concomitant variation extending over continuous regions of space of time. . . . The unit of time is essentially modifiable.

. . .

Our correlations will accordingly measure the relationship between variates *for the specified units chosen for the work*. They have no absolute validity independently of those units, but are relative to them. They measure, as it were, not only the variation of the quantities under consideration, but the properties of the unit-mesh which we have imposed on the system in order to measure it. [Yule and Kendall 1950, p. 312]

This distinction has intuitive appeal and seems to convey something of the difficulty involved in shifting levels of analysis in empirical research. Yet the distinction between modifiable and nonmodifiable units does not appear to be a useful practical guide. It is not clear what unit if any would be non-modifiable. As Galtung [1967] points out, even the individual is not an indivisible unit when viewed from the perspective of a social actor adopting multiple roles. Further, what to some analysts are simple behavioral acts may be seen from the perspective of other theories as instances of complex cognitive and physiological processes. The problem is quite general. The meaningfulness of units as well as their modifiability can be judged only in relation to a substantive theory.

This is certainly true in the case of areal groupings of observations. To those employing theories which do not specifically incorporate structural variables in microprocesses (e.g., those investigating what Homans [1961] calls "elementary laws" of social behavior), any areal grouping of behavioral observations is likely to appear arbitrary and highly modifiable. The same is not the case when structural variables which are related to the unit employed enter the theoretical formulation. For example, if one is concerned with political processes which are assumed to occur only in independent polities (i.e., units that are ultimately sovereign with respect to control over certain functions), areal units which coincide with political jurisdictions will not be considered either arbitrary or modifiable.

Since we reject this distinction as a useful methodological guide, we must offer an alternative. Our procedure is to focus (1) on the substantive significance of what we have called earlier the aggregation relations and (2) on more general relations which express the relations of the microvariables to all macrovariables (introduced in Chapter 5 as "auxiliary regressions"). Since we have not introduced all of the basic analysis needed to discuss these relations, we delay further discussion to later sections.

Yule and Kendall go on to explain the inflation of correlation co-efficients, in terms of the effects of grouping, on random components in variables. This analysis is somewhat imprecise and misleading.[1] Considerably more insight can be gained from applications of analysis of covariance thinking. Thus, we turn now to this approach.

Results from the Analysis of Covariance

Sociologists have made considerable headway in unraveling aggregation–disaggregation effects by formulating the problems in terms of an analysis of covariance design. Robinson's [1950] seminal paper on this topic begins with "the fundamental theorem from the analysis of covariance" (which is never explicitly stated). Duncan, Cuzzort, and Duncan [1961] systematized and extended his analysis by making explicit the connections between the "ecological fallacy" and results from the analysis of covariance. Recently, there has been something of an upsurge of interest in this application of covariance analysis.[2]

Since the arguments are quite central it is useful to develop the analysis model at some length. For the present, we restrict our attention to a pair of variables X and Y on which we have N microobservations. We model the aggregation relations by assuming that these N observations are grouped into R exhaustive subsets, each subset containing N_r microobservations. These aggregates have typically been thought of as areal groupings of micro-observations. We may, as discussed above, consider these subsets as more general partitions existing in the social structure, e.g., age, organizational membership, class in school, etc. To make clear the formal identity of areal aggregation with temporal aggregation we explicitly introduce a temporal dimension. Each microobservation is indexed by time of observation where we have T time periods. Thus, each microobservation X_{irt} and Y_{irt} should be thought of as the value for the variable X or Y for microunit i in aggregate r at time t. We employ this notation along with the familiar "dot" summation notation, that is,

$$X. = \sum_i X_i$$

to represent averages taken over microunits, groupings, and time periods. These notations are presented in Table 3-2, which follows the organization of Alker [1969].

---

[1] This analysis is summarized by Hannan [1970a, ch. 2].

[2] See Fennessey [1968], Schuessler [1969], Alker [1969], and Slatin [1970].

To obtain covariance theorems, we manipulate several decompositions of deviation terms. We can state on the basis of the definitions in the table that

$$(X_{irt} - X_{\cdot t}) = (X_{irt} - X_{\cdot rt}) + (X_{\cdot rt} - X_{\cdot t}) \tag{3.1}$$

or a slightly more complex version:

$$(X_{irt} - X_{\cdot \cdot}) = (X_{irt} - X_{\cdot rt}) + (X_{\cdot rt} - X_{\cdot t}) + (X_{\cdot t} - X_{\cdot \cdot}) \tag{3.2}$$

Equation (3.2) gives a time-specific decomposition of the moment of X_{irt} in terms of within-aggregate, between-aggregate, and overall deviations. That is, the deviation of any microobservation from the overall mean can be expressed as a sum of deviations: the deviation of the microobservation from the group average for the time-period average (of all aggregations), and the deviation of the latter from the overall mean.

If we sum equations (3.1) and (3.2) over t, we obtain the following simple result:

$$(X_{i\cdot} - X_{\cdot \cdot}) = (X_{i\cdot} - X_{\cdot r\cdot}) + (X_{\cdot r\cdot} - X_{\cdot \cdot}) \tag{3.3}$$

By ignoring time, we can obtain the result usually encountered in introductory statistics courses.

$$(X_i - X_\cdot) = (X_i - X_{\cdot r}) + (X_{\cdot r} - X_\cdot) \tag{3.4}$$

This expresses an overall deviation as a sum of an individual deviation and an aggregate deviation. Alker [1969, p. 74] notes that by subtracting equation (3.3) from equation (3.1) and rearranging we can obtain the more complex but potentially useful expression

$$\underbrace{(X_{irt} - X_{i\cdot})}_{\text{total trend}} = \underbrace{(X_{irt} - X_{\cdot rt}) - (X_{i\cdot} - X_{\cdot r\cdot})}_{\text{individual trend}}$$

$$+ \underbrace{(X_{\cdot rt} - X_{\cdot t}) - (X_{\cdot r\cdot} - X_{\cdot \cdot})}_{\text{aggregate trend}} + \underbrace{(X_{\cdot t} - X_{\cdot \cdot})}_{\text{overall trend}} \tag{3.5}$$

The first covariance theorems can be derived from equation (3.1) by multiplying corresponding expressions for $(X_{irt} - X_{\cdot t})$ and $Y_{irt} - Y_{\cdot t})$ and averaging over all units in all aggregations:

$$\frac{1}{N_r} \sum_{r=1}^{R} \sum_{i=1}^{N_r} (X_{irt} - X_{\cdot t})(Y_{irt} - Y_{\cdot t})$$

$$= \frac{1}{N_r} \sum_{r=1}^{R} \sum_{i=1}^{N_r} (X_{irt} - X_{\cdot rt})(Y_{irt} - Y_{\cdot rt}) + \frac{1}{N_r} \sum_{r=1}^{R} \sum_{i=1}^{N_r} (X_{\cdot rt} - X_{\cdot t})(Y_{\cdot rt} - Y_{\cdot t})$$

$$+ \frac{1}{N_r} \sum_{r=1}^{R} \sum_{i=1}^{N_r} (X_{irt} - X_{\cdot rt})(Y_{\cdot rt} - Y_{\cdot t}) + \frac{1}{N_r} \sum_{r=1}^{R} \sum_{i=1}^{N_r} (X_{\cdot rt} - X_{\cdot t})(Y_{irt} - Y_{\cdot rt})$$

Table 3–2. Statistical Elements of Covariance Theorems

Symbol	Computational Formula	Interpretation
(A1) X_{irt}, Y_{irt}	$i = 1, \ldots, N; r = 1, \ldots, R;$ $N_1 + \cdots + N_r + \cdots + N_R = N;$ $t = 1, \ldots, T$	The value of variable X (or Y) at time t for unit i belonging to aggregate r
(A2) $X_{\cdot rt}$	$\dfrac{1}{N_r} \displaystyle\sum_{i=1}^{N_r} X_{irt}; \left(\displaystyle\sum_{r=1}^{R} N_r = N \right)$	The average value of X at time t for all N_r units i belonging to aggregate r
(A3) $X_{\cdot t}$	$\dfrac{1}{N} \displaystyle\sum_{r=1}^{R} \sum_{i=1}^{N_r} X_{irt}$	The average value of X at time t for all N units
(A4) $X_{i\cdot}$	$\dfrac{1}{T} \displaystyle\sum_{t=1}^{T} X_{irt}$	The average value of X for all times t for a particular unit i
(A5) $X_{\cdot r}$	$\dfrac{1}{TN_r} \displaystyle\sum_{t=1}^{T} \sum_{i=1}^{N_r} X_{irt}$	The average value of X for all units i belonging to aggregate r and all times t
(A6) $X_{\cdot\cdot}$	$\dfrac{1}{TN_r} \displaystyle\sum_{t=1}^{T} \sum_{r=1}^{R} \sum_{i=1}^{N_r} X_{irt}$	The average value of X for all units i and times t

Formulas exactly parallel to (A2) through (A6) hold for $Y_{\cdot rt}$, $Y_{\cdot t}$, $Y_{\cdot r}$, and $Y_{\cdot\cdot}$.

(B1) $C_{XY;t}$	$\dfrac{1}{N} \displaystyle\sum_{r=1}^{R} \sum_{i=1}^{N_r} (X_{irt} - X_{\cdot t})(Y_{irt} - Y_{\cdot t})$	The overall covariance of X and Y for all units i (at time t)
(B2) C_{XY}	$\dfrac{1}{TN} \displaystyle\sum_{t=1}^{T} \sum_{r=1}^{R} \sum_{i=1}^{N_r} (X_{irt} - X_{\cdot\cdot})(Y_{irt} - Y_{\cdot\cdot})$	The overall covariance of X and Y for all i and t
(B3) $C_{XX;t}$	$\dfrac{1}{N} \displaystyle\sum_{r=1}^{R} \sum_{i=1}^{N_r} (X_{irt} - X_{\cdot t})^2$	The overall variance of X for all units i (at time t)

(A similar expression with double sums and deviations about $X_{\cdot\cdot}$, gives C_{XX})

(B4) $WC_{XY;t}$	$\dfrac{1}{N} \displaystyle\sum_{r=1}^{R} \sum_{i=1}^{N_r} (X_{irt} - X_{\cdot rt})(Y_{irt} - Y_{\cdot rt})$	The within-aggregate covariance of X and Y (at time t)

Similarly, with double sums and deviations, etc. we can define WC_{XY})

(B5) $C_{XYr;t}$	$\dfrac{1}{N_r} \displaystyle\sum_{i=1}^{N_r} (X_{irt} - X_{\cdot rt})(Y_{irt} - Y_{\cdot rt})$	The covariance of X and Y within a particular aggregate r (at time t)
(B6) $EC_{XY;t}$	$\dfrac{1}{N} \displaystyle\sum_{r=1}^{R} \sum_{i=1}^{N_r} (X_{\cdot rt} - X_{\cdot t})(Y_{\cdot rt} - Y_{\cdot t})$	The between-aggregate or "ecological" covariance of X and Y (at time t)

(Similarly, we may define, EC_{XY})

(B7) TC_{XY}	$\dfrac{1}{TN} \displaystyle\sum_{t=1}^{T} \sum_{r=1}^{R} \sum_{i=1}^{N_r} (X_{\cdot t} - X_{\cdot\cdot})(Y_{\cdot t} - Y_{\cdot\cdot})$	The between-times or "trend" covariance of X and Y

(B8) $WC_{XX;t}$ $\dfrac{1}{N} \displaystyle\sum_{r=1}^{R} \sum_{i=1}^{N_r} (X_{irt} - X_{\cdot rt})^2$ The "within-aggregate" variance of X (at time t)

(Similarly, with double sums and deviations about $X_{\cdot r\cdot}$, we can define WC_{XX})

(B9) $EC_{XX;t}$ $\dfrac{1}{N} \displaystyle\sum_{r=1}^{R} \sum_{i=1}^{N_r} (X_{\cdot rt} - X_{\cdot t})^2$ The between-aggregate or "ecological" variance of X (at time t)

(Similarly, we may define EC_{XY})

Formulas analogous to (B3), (B8), and (B9) hold for $C_{YY;t}$, $WC_{YY;t}$, $EC_{YY;t}$; and C_{YY}, WC_{YY}, and EC_{YY}.

(C1) $E^2_{XR;t}$ $\dfrac{EC_{XX;t}}{C_{YY;t}}$ The correlation ratio of X and R (at time t)

(C2) $E^2_{YR;t}$ $\dfrac{EC_{YY;t}}{C_{YY;t}}$ The correlation ratio of Y and R (at time t)

(D1) $R_{XY;t}$ $\left(\dfrac{C_{XY;t}}{C_{XX;t}\,C_{YY;t}}\right)^{1/2}$ The overall correlation of X and Y (at time t)

(D2) $WR_{XY;t}$ $\left(\dfrac{WC_{XY;t}}{WC_{XX;t}\,WC_{YY;t}}\right)^{1/2}$ The within-aggregate correlation of X and Y (at time t)

(D3) $ER_{XY;t}$ $\left(\dfrac{EC_{XY;t}}{EC_{XX;t}\,EC_{YY;t}}\right)^{1/2}$ The between-aggregate or "ecological" correlation of X and Y (at time t)

After time-averaging, formulas (D1) through (D3) give R_{XY}, WR_{XY}, or ER_{XY}.

Fortunately, when we multiply the terms out and sum the resulting terms—the last two terms on the right-hand side (the cross-level covariances)—cancel each other out.[3] In terms of the covariance notation and definitional formulas (B1), (B4), and (B6), the remaining terms can be written:

$$C_{XY;t} = WC_{XY;t} + EC_{XY;t} \qquad (3.6)$$

In other words, the covariance between X and Y for N microunits i at a specific time t can be represented as the sum of a within-aggregate covariance and a between-aggregate or ecological covariance for the same time t. As the

[3] As Alker notes, it is helpful in showing this cancellation to remember that the r subscripts refer to various specific subsets of i, and that the averages over all i are equivalent to proportionally weighted combinations of dot-r averages.

preceding derivation (and the definitional formulas) make clear, the between-aggregate covariance can be thought of as a population-weighted sum over all regions of the covariances of micro X and Y values within each of the aggregates; and similarly, the ecological covariance is a population-weighted averaged (expected) product of the deviations of aggregates in X and Y.

Alker goes on to derive a more complex and less familiar form of the covariance theorem from a similar treatment of equation (3.2):

$$C_{XY} = WC_{XY} + EC_{XY} + TC_{XY} \tag{3.7}$$

This expression decomposes the covariance over i and t of X_{irt} and Y_{irt} into temporally averaged within- and between-aggregate terms and a trend component.

To obtain the correlational version of the covariance theorem used by Robinson, we simply divide covariance terms by standard deviations to obtain correlations—as can be seen in Table 3-2, (C1) and (C2). We obtain:

$$R_{XY} = \frac{WC_{XY} + EC_{XY}}{\sqrt{C_{XX}C_{YY}}}$$

$$= \frac{WC_{XY}}{\sqrt{WC_{XX}WC_{YY}}} \cdot \sqrt{\frac{WC_{XX}WC_{YY}}{C_{XX}C_{YY}}} + \frac{EC_{XY}}{\sqrt{EC_{XX}EC_{YY}}} \cdot \sqrt{\frac{EC_{XX}EC_{YY}}{C_{XX}C_{YY}}}$$

We can make substitutions from the formulas of Table 3–2 still ignoring time-specific subscripts (and recalling that $WC_{XX} = C_{XX} - EC_{XX}$ and $WC_{YY} = C_{YY} - EC_{YY}$) to arrive at the formulation of the covariance theorem that Robinson used:

$$R_{XY} = WR_{XY}\sqrt{1 - E_{YR}^2}\sqrt{1 - E_{XR}^2} + ER_{XY}E_{YR}E_{XR} \tag{3.8}$$

Employing a similar strategy, Duncan, Cuzzort, and Duncan [1961] derived the following result for slopes:

$$B_{YX} = WB_{YX} + E_{XR}^2(EB_{YX} - WB_{YX}) \tag{3.9}$$

These authors stress two points relative to both the above results: first, the within-aggregate coefficients, WR_{XY} and WB_{YX}, are not simple weighted sums of the total (microlevel) coefficients, R_{XY} and B_{YX}. That is, we do not obtain these coefficients by calculating an average microcorrelation for each aggregate and summing these averages (weighted by observations in the aggregate). Instead, WR_{XY} and WB_{YX} are computed from sums of squares and products pooled over all aggregations before performing multiplication, square root extraction, or the division involved in the computations. In other words, these coefficients depend on the entire patterning of the partition in aggregates, not merely on the microlevel coefficients categorized by aggregates. And second, it is not possible to express the microcorrelation and regression coefficients solely as functions of the corresponding parameter estimates computed on aggregates. Equations (3.8) and (3.9) make it clear that this relationship depends as we have already noted on the within-aggregate coefficients and on the correlation ratios.

W. Ș. Robinson [1950] used equation (3.8) to explain the grouping effect on correlations. Equation (3.8) can be rearranged and simplified in the form:

$$ER_{XY} = \frac{R_{XY}}{E_{XR}E_{YR}} - \frac{WR_{XY}\sqrt{1 - E_{XR}^2}\sqrt{1 - E_{YR}^2}}{E_{XR}E_{YR}} \qquad (3.10)$$

From this Robinson deduced an *equivalency assumption* (ecological correlation equal to the total or individual correlation):

$$WR_{XY} = \frac{R_{XY}(1 - E_{XR}E_{YR})}{\sqrt{1 - E_{XR}^2}\sqrt{1 - E_{YR}^2}} \quad \text{or} \quad WR_{XY} = kR_{XY} \qquad (3.11)$$

The two correlations are equal only if the equality holds. The minimum value of k in the abbreviated expression is unity. This is the case in which the within-aggregate correlation is exactly equal to the microcorrelation. This is the limiting case of the first point made by Duncan, Cuzzort, and Duncan in which the within-aggregate correlation is simply a weighted average of the microcorrelations across aggregates. As we will see, this is unlikely in interesting cases. Robinson [1950, p. 356] argues, "The correlation between X and Y is certainly not larger for the relatively homogeneous subgroups than it is for the population at large." But, unstated in this argument is the postulate that the magnitude of a correlation coefficient is dependent on the range of variation of the independent variable. If this range of variation is restricted (as we would expect it to be when some homogeneous subgroup of population is selected out), the correlation will be attenuated.

Robinson proceeded to point out that an examination of equation (3.11) shows why the ecological correlation depends on the level of aggregation. As smaller aggregates are consolidated, two things happen:

1. The within-aggregation correlation, WR_{XY}, increases as a result of increasing heterogeneity of the more inclusive aggregates; and this effect decreases the ecological correlation, since the proportion of variance explained by "the aggregate" is equal to $1 - WR_{XY}^2$.
2. The values of the correlation ratios, E_{XR} and E_{YR}, decrease as a result of the decrease in the heterogeneity of values of A and Y in the aggregates.

The effect of these changes is to increase the ecological correlation.

However, these two tendencies are of unequal importance. Investigation of (3.11) with respect to the effect of changes in the values of E_{XR}, E_{YR}, and WR_{XY} indicates that the influence of the changes in the E's is considerably more important than the influence of changes in the value of WR_{XY}. The net effect of changes in the E's and WR_{XY} taken together is to increase the numerical value of the ecological correlation as consolidation takes place. [Robinson 1950, pp. 356–357]

The point, again, is that grouping units somehow changes the variation in the variables being analyzed. Exactly how grouping or aggregation affects variation in such variables became much clearer when Blalock [1964] considered the issue in the context of linear causal analysis.

A Causal Perspective

It is clear by now that we must concern ourselves with the effects of aggregation on all of the variables in the substantive model. Blalock has made this issue the explicit focus of his treatment of the problem of changing units of analysis. He argues:

. . . in shifting from one unit of analysis to another we are very likely to affect the manner in which outside and potentially disturbing influences are operating on the dependent and independent variables under consideration. [Blalock 1964, p. 98]

The way in which this is likely to occur is that variation in X or Y or both may be manipulated in such a way that their variation becomes confounded with variation in other variables either included or excluded from the model. The key insight is that the effect of shifting levels of analysis on the behavior of correlation and regression coefficients depends on the manner in which the units (microobservations) have been put together. If we explicitly consider the aggregation or grouping criterion (or, in some more complicated cases, criteria) as a variable in the model, we can begin to see the effects of given kinds of aggregation on the variation in the variables of interest. We have already noted, for example, that grouping by area of residence (spatial location) will tend to maximize variation in many social variables (i.e., will tend to increase between-group variation relative to within-group variation). As Blalock points out, however, we seldom have precise information on the connections between the aggregation criterion and the theoretically meaningful variables in the model.

In order to gain some insight into the likely effects of several different types of grouping procedures on bivariate correlation and regression coefficients, Blalock examined the effects of four grouping procedures on the relationship between percent nonwhite and economic discrimination in 150 Southern counties. The four procedure types were random grouping, grouping maximizing variation in X (the independent variable), grouping maximizing variation in Y (the dependent variable), and proximity grouping. The first three are "artificial" groupings while the fourth corresponds to the case we have considered to this point.

Blalock considered the effects of the four types of grouping or aggregation on the coefficients b_{yx}, b_{xy}, and r_{xy} in the simple model pictured in Figure 3-1. The lack of arrows connecting either W or Z with X indicates that these former variables are causes of Y which are unrelated to X. As a heuristic device, we will introduce a new variable (A) into the model to represent the grouping criterion and will make explicit by means of arrows the relationship of (A) to the other variables in the model.

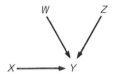

Figure 3-1. A Simple Bivariate Causal Model with Two Latent Variables (W and Z).

The case of random grouping where X and Y observations are put together randomly can be represented as in Figure 3-2. Blalock notes that Laws-of-Large-Numbers arguments suggest that variation in all variables should be reduced by purely random grouping. Thus, we would expect X to explain the same proportion of variation in Y at all levels of grouping and the value of r_{xy} to remain unchanged except for sampling fluctuations. Formulas developed by Goodman [1959] also suggest that the covariation of the two variables should decrease in the same proportion as the variation in X and Y and thus the expected value of the regression coefficients should be unchanged. Blalock's manipulations supported these predictions.

In the second procedure, units with similar X values were grouped together into successively larger and larger aggregates. Such grouping maximizes the between-groups variation in X relative to the within-groups variation. Since W and Z are assumed to be unrelated to X, this procedure operates randomly with respect to these variables. As a result, variation in X relative to variation in W and Z (and all other causes of Y which are independent of X) is increased, and X accordingly explains a larger proportion of the

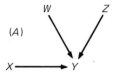

Figure 3–2. Example of a Grouping Criterion Which Is Independent of Variables in the Model.

variation in Y. However, the slope of this relationship, b_{yx}, should be unaffected by such a grouping procedure; although, as we will see later, this grouping reduces the efficiency of the slope estimate. Progressively more inclusive groupings of Blalock's county data in this way produced consistent increases in the correlation coefficient and left the slope relatively unchanged. The causal mechanism operating in such a grouping procedure can be abstracted and diagrammed as in Figure 3-3.

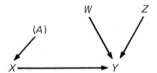

Figure 3–3. Grouping by the Independent Variable.

Blalock then employed such a systematic grouping strategy on Y, the dependent variable. It would seem plausible, on the basis of the argument just made, to suspect that X would explain a smaller percentage of the variation in Y in this case. However, r_{xy} behaves symmetrically with respect to X and Y and increases when variation in either variable is maximized. In addition, the slope of interest (since the model takes Y to be the dependent variable), b_{yx}, increases. This can be considered a mathematical artifact. As in the previous kind of grouping, the slope b_{yx} remains relatively constant while r_{xy} increases with consolidation. Since $r_{xy}^2 = b_{yx}b_{xy}$, b_{yx} must increase proportionately with increases in the squared correlation coefficient. In causal terms, we can explain this as a confounding of the effects of variables such as W and Z with the effects of X. Blalock notes that when we group systematically by Y, we will put together very high values of Y; and in another group we will put together very low values of Y, etc. If we assume without loss of generality that X, W, and Z are all positively related to Y, we would assume that very high Y values would occur as a result of high values of X, W, and Z. Thus, in such a grouping procedure one would be grouping units with high values of X, W, and Z together even when there is no tendency for such variables to be correlated in the population of interest. Blalock [1964, p. 108] presents an example of this effect. Two explanatory variables which are moderately correlated with the dependent variable and only weakly correlated with each other (.08) become highly correlated with grouping by the dependent variable. The net result is that it becomes impossible to disentangle the effects of X from the effects of other variables related to the dependent variable. This situation is diagrammed in Figure 3-4.

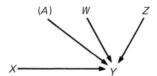

Figure 3-4. Grouping by the Dependent Variable.

Blalock then grouped county units on the basis of geographical proximity into progressively more inclusive aggregates. In this case, the numerical value of r_{xy} increased with the level of grouping while the value of the slope remained relatively unchanged. Thus, for this body of data it appears that proximity grouping constituted a procedure intermediate between random grouping and grouping maximizing variation in the independent variable of interest. However, in any instance it is an empirical question whether or not proximity (including both spatial and temporal) grouping will have more effect on variation in X or Y. We have implied above that many of the variables of interest to social scientists are likely to be clustered spatially and temporally. If this is the case, a more realistic model is probably more like that presented in Figure 3-5 which is a composite of the models from Figures 3-3 and 3-4 with additional arrows drawn from (A) to the other causal factors. The issue then becomes one of the relative importance of the many connections between the grouping criterion and the variables in the model. In Blalock's particular example of proximity grouping, it is apparently the case that the relationship of (A) and X is stronger than the relations of (A) with W, Z, or Y.

The model drawn in Figure 3-5 raises a very interesting possibility, the possibility of the grouping criterion producing a spurious relationship between

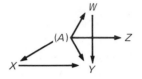

Figure 3–5. Grouping Which Affects All Variables.

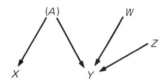

Figure 3–6. Spurious Macrocorrelation.

X and Y. Consider the model drawn in Figure 3-6. In such a case we would expect to find no relationship between X and Y at the microlevel; but, at the macrolevel such a relationship would appear due to the operation of the grouping procedure. This important possibility seems to have been overlooked until very recently in the aggregation literature. Alker [1969] has raised the issue and suggests that the literature on ecological correlations would have developed quite differently if those who addressed the problem had explicitly considered the problem of spuriousness.

It is useful to pursue Alker's example. Recall that Robinson found an individual correlation of .20 between race and literacy, while the correlation computed on census district marginals was .95. We are interested in controlling for "region," the grouping criterion, in the model drawn in Figure 3-6. Following Alker, we can use equation (3.7) developed above. We have

$$.20 = WR_{XY} \sqrt{1 - E_{XA}^2} \sqrt{1 - E_{YA}^2} + .95E_{XA}E_{YA}$$

If we make the rather plausible assumption that half of the variance in each variable is accounted for by region, i.e., $E_{XA}^2 = E_{YA}^2 = .25$, we obtain

$$.20 = .75WR_{XY} + .24$$

from which we deduce $WR_{XY} = -.05$. In other words, the control for region here reduces an individual correlation which is nonzero as well as a large ecological correlation to (approximately) zero. Note that this result is dependent on the correlation ratio assumptions and that we would not normally have access to both the micro- and macrocorrelations.

How is this result to be explained? Alker suggests that the operative factor in the regional grouping variable may have been level of industrialization, i.e., in grouping microobservations according to region (or level of industrialization of region of residence) we tend to group units which are high on literacy and have low nonwhite populations, or the reverse, when there is no causal relationship connecting race and literacy.

It would seem that the possibility of the problem just discussed in any concrete aggregation problem could be evaluated only by a detailed knowledge of the data being employed. This seems a difficult but tractable problem. But what of the situation when there is likely to be a substantively interesting causal relation between the aggregation criterion and one or more variables of interest? Without a theory specifying such relations, we would face an overwhelming range of choices of causal specifications of such relations in any fairly complex situation. This problem seems to point to a real need, in the face of aggregation–disaggregation problems, of *cross-level theories*. If we had such theories, we would be in a better position to uncover the various biasing aggregation problems discussed to this point. Better yet, we would be able to explicitly include the operative variable(s) masked under a surrogate variable (like region) in the model. This would seem to be the obvious direction of movement in dealing with many of the problems raised by Blalock.

The need for cross-level theories becomes more obvious as we consider more complex models, say five- or six-variable recursive models. It seems likely that a grouping criterion as broad and as amorphous as region (or time period of occurrence) could be a surrogate for a large number of possible causal influences, e.g., level of industrialization, political structure, cultural factors, etc. It is obvious that the crucial step in resolving many aggregation problems will involve determining which of the many possible causal factors are in fact operating in such a situation and how exactly such influences differentially affect the variation in variables of immediate interest. *The simple notion of a clustering effect is shown by a causal analysis to be too undifferentiated to be of much help in resolving the problems.*

Finally, we can note that in complex models, aggregation is likely to give rise to a number of simultaneous complications. Among the complications possible are those already discussed, controlling for dependent variables, and the production of spurious relationships, as well as controlling for prior variables in causal chains. In the fifth chapter we will briefly consider some of the additional complications that may arise when multivariate models are estimated over a time series of observations.

Aggregation and Efficiency

We have seen that aggregation which operates directly on the independent variables does not bias least squares estimates. This is an encouraging result. However, it is not widely known to sociologists that such *aggregation produces a reduction in the efficiency of the least squares estimators*. We do, then, pay some price for the simplicity and ease of analysis gained through aggregation. The following proof is due to Cramer [1964].

We begin with a classical ordinary regression model. We assume fixed (nonstochastic) values of the explanatory variable (although the results are generalizable to drawings from a bivariate normal population) with additive disturbances which are independent drawings from a normal population with mean zero and variance, and which are independent of the x_{ir}. Thus,

$$Y_{ir} = \alpha + \beta X_{ir} + U_{ir} \tag{3.12}$$

where we continue to employ subscripts in the same way as above.

In the following we deal with sums of squares and cross-products rather than with the corresponding variance and covariance terms. Accordingly we will use the following notation for these quantities:

$$S_{xx} = \sum_{r=1}^{R} \sum_{i=1}^{N_r} (X_{ir} - X..)^2 \tag{3.13}$$

$$S_{xu} = \sum_{r=1}^{R} \sum_{i=1}^{N_r} (X_{ir} - X..)(U_{ir} - U..) \tag{3.14}$$

and so forth. The corresponding terms calculated from the weighted aggregate means are

$$BS_{xx} = \sum_{r=1}^{R} N_r (X._r - X..)^2 \tag{3.15}$$

$$BS_{xu} = \sum_{r=1}^{R} N_r (X._r - X..)(U._r - U..) \tag{3.16}$$

and so forth. The within-group sums of squares and cross-products are similarly defined. As we saw above, in the case of covariances we may form a partition:

$$S_{xx} = BS_{xx} + WS_{xx} \tag{3.17}$$

and similarly,

$$S_{xu} = BS_{xu} + WS_{xu} \tag{3.18}$$

If we substitute equation (3.12) into the cross-product S_{xy}, we obtain

$$S_{xy} = \beta S_{xx} + S_{xu} \tag{3.19}$$

and for weighted group means

$$BS_{xy} = \beta BS_{xx} + BS_{xu} \tag{3.20}$$

We focus our attention on the disturbance terms in equations (3.19) and (3.20). We noted in equation (3.18) that $S_{xu} = BS_{xu} + WS_{xu}$. This is a partition of a (weighted) sum of normally distributed random variables into two independent parts. Since the original distribution is normal with mean zero, each of the resulting independent distributions is normal with mean zero. Thus

$$E(S_{xu}) = 0, \qquad E(BS_{xu}) = 0, \qquad E(WS_{xu}) = 0 \tag{3.21}$$

and the variances are as follows:

$$\text{var}(S_{xu}) = S_{xx}\sigma_u^2, \qquad \text{var}(BS_{xu}) = BS_{xx}\sigma_u^2, \qquad \text{var}(WS_{xu}) = WS_{xx}\sigma_u^2 \tag{3.22}$$

Given that the two terms on the right-hand side of equation (3.18), BS_{xu} and WS_{xu}, are independent,

$$\text{cov}(BS_{xu}, WS_{xu}) = 0$$

Hence,

$$\text{cov}(S_{xu}, BS_{xu}) = \text{var}(BS_{xu}) = BS_{xx}\sigma_u^2 \tag{3.23}$$

Cramer uses these results to consider the aggregate or grouped bivariate regression coefficient. The microlevel regression coefficient is defined as

$$b = \frac{S_{xy}}{S_{xx}} \tag{3.24}$$

and the regression coefficient for weighted group means is

$$b' = \frac{BS_{xy}}{BS_{xx}} \tag{3.25}$$

Now we can use the earlier results to obtain some interesting identities. Substituting (3.19) into (3.24) we obtain

$$b = \beta + \frac{S_{xu}}{S_{xx}} \tag{3.26}$$

and substituting (3.20) into (3.25) gives

$$b' = \beta + \frac{BS_{xu}}{BS_{xx}} \tag{3.27}$$

Making use of the properties of the disturbance term, see (3.11), we find that

$$E(b) = \beta, \qquad E(b') = \beta \tag{3.28}$$

Thus, when we group units according to values of the independent variable, aggregate least squares produces an unbiased estimate of the slope.

Cramer does not mention the case in which the grouping process minimizes variation in the dependent variable. As Blalock demonstrates, such a procedure confounds variation in x with variation in u. We can see the consequence of this in Cramer's formulation. When variation in the explanatory variable becomes confounded with the residual, the term BX_{xu} no longer has zero expected value and the expected value of b' does not reduce to β. More abstractly, we can think of this bias as a case of specification bias. Ordinary least squares produces unbiased slope estimates only when the explanatory variables are independent of the disturbance or residual terms. Grouping by the dependent variable produces a macromodel in which this requirement is violated. Thus, it is not surprising that aggregation bias results.

Shively [1969] proves that for aggregation in percentage tables (to be discussed in Chapter 4), the bias resulting from grouping by the dependent variable must inflate the absolute value of the slope, i.e., when the microslope is positive the aggregation bias is positive and when the microslope is negative the aggregation bias is negative. This result depends on the specification of the attainment of maxima and minima (which are easily defined for percentages). Examination of what we have identified as the bias term in equation (3.27) suggests a ready extension to the continuous-variable case. Since BS_{xx} is by definition a nonnegative quantity, the direction of the aggregation bias depends solely on the sign of BS_{xu}. Following Blalock's analysis (reported above), it is easy to specify its sign for relatively simple cases. Consider the case where β is positive. To obtain high y_{ir} values, we would have to obtain high values of both x_{ir} and u_{ir}. Thus, grouping by y will produce a positive covariance between x and u. The aggregation bias then is positive. A similar analysis for negative β demonstrates a symmetric aggregation bias. This result holds for more complicated recursive models (although as we pointed out previously it is not often easy to specify simple aggregation effects in such models).

A second argument by Shively concerns the decrease of the mangitude of aggregation bias, in this case with increases in the "strength" (in the explained variance sense) of the microrelation. We can see again in equation (3.27) support for this contention. As the proportion of variance in y which is not linearly accountable for by x decreases in this model, BS_{xu} will decrease relative to BS_{xx}. Or, in the perspective adopted above, the specification error produces less bias when the residual term is small in effect.

We can demonstrate that aggregation or grouping according to the independent variable does increase the variance of the slope estimator.

(Kmenta [1971] demonstrates that aggregation also produces heteroscedasticity when the groupings depend on unequal numbers of microobservations.) From equations (3.26) and (3.27) we have

$$(b - \beta) = \frac{S_{xu}}{S_{xx}} \quad \text{and} \quad (b' - \beta) = \frac{BS_{xu}}{BS_{xx}}$$

so that by (3.22) we can deduce

$$\text{var}(b) = \frac{\sigma_u^2}{S_{xx}} \quad \text{and} \quad \text{var}(b') = \frac{\sigma_u^2}{BS_{xx}} \qquad (3.29)$$

The effect of this type of grouping is to increase the variance of the slope estimate by a factor

$$\frac{S_{xx}}{BS_{xx}} \qquad (3.30)$$

Thus, we can say that this ratio expresses the difference in the variance of the slope estimates at the two levels of aggregation. As the argument suggests, if we have a choice of several unbiased estimators, we generally wish to base this choice on their relative efficiency. If $\hat{\theta}_1$ and $\hat{\theta}_2$ are two unbiased estimators of some parameter θ, $\hat{\theta}_1$ is said to be more efficient than $\hat{\theta}_2$ if the $\text{var}(\hat{\theta}_1)$ is less than the $\text{var}(\hat{\theta}_2)$. The measure of relative efficiency is thus given by $\text{var}(\hat{\theta}_2)/\text{var}(\hat{\theta}_1)$. Estimators with small variance are desirable because their distributions tend as a result of this fact to be more highly concentrated around the parameter of interest than will be the case with estimators with greater variances. In particular, *grouping the independent variable reduces the efficiency of estimation by the inverse function*

$$\frac{BS_{xx}}{S_{xx}} \qquad (3.31)$$

Since the terms involved in this ratio, sums of squares, are nonnegative, the measure of loss of efficiency (3.31) is nonnegative. The closer this ratio is to unity, the less the difference in relative efficiency at the two levels, the less does grouping the independent variable increase the variance of the slope estimate.

It follows from this analysis that if a researcher had control over aggregation procedures, he would be wise to choose a strategy that will maximize the ratio (3.31). Examination of the partition (3.17) shows that this is equivalent to maximizing the between-group variation relative to the within-group variation in x. This result, then, is congruent with Blalock's formulation.

To further stress the parallel with Blalock's treatment, it is interesting to consider Cramer's analysis of random grouping. With this type of grouping, we obtain an unbiased estimate of the regression coefficient with a variance of say, σ_u^2/S_{xx}^*, where S_{xx}^* is either the weighted between-aggregate sums of squares for R random aggregates or the sum of squares of R microobservations taken at random (since the expected value of the two are equal). Since the grouping is random the between-group variance should exactly equal the within-group variance apart from the corrections for degrees of freedom, $R - 1$ and $N - 1$ respectively. If we express the loss of efficiency as in (3.31), we obtain a ratio on the order of

$$\frac{R - 1}{N - 1} \tag{3.32}$$

Here the loss of efficiency depends solely on the number of groups or aggregates created. The fewer the number of groupings, the greater the loss of efficiency. This result accords with intuition since as the number of groups increases, R approaches N and we lose less and less information using aggregates rather than the whole sample or population.

To this point we have considered only the true variance of the estimators at the different levels. Cramer goes on to demonstrate that when we examine the sampling variance of the slope estimate at the two levels (which we must use to test hypotheses about β), we again find that the estimate from grouped data is much more variable than the estimate computed from individual data.

Aggregation and Spectral Analysis

Earlier in this chapter, we used a covariance model to suggest the formal similarity of areal and temporal aggregation. We can further support this argument by citing an interesting application of time series analysis techniques to the aggregation problem. The technique involved is called spectral analysis and is widely used in a number of sciences in the study of temporal processes. The mathematics are quite complicated and thus we will not develop the arguments extensively.[4]

A ubiquitous concern in the analysis of time-varying behavior is the nature of the dependence of present or future states of a process on earlier states. One way of representing such dependence is to calculate *autocorrelations* which express the linear association of temporally spaced states of some process. That is, if we have a process $X(t)$ with finite mean $\mu(t)$, the

---

[4] See Fishman [1969] for a lucid introduction.

autocovariance function for the observations at time s and t, $R(s, t)$ takes the following form:

$$R(s, t) = E[X(s) - \mu(s)][X(t) - \mu(t)]$$

The normalized version, the autocorrelation denoted $\rho(s, t)$ is

$$\rho(s, t) = \frac{R(s, t)}{[R(s, s)R(t, t)]^{1/2}}$$

where $R(s, s)$ is the variance of the process at time s.

In previous analyses we noted the widely employed assumption that states of a process which are "close together" in time are more highly correlated than those separated by a greater time interval. It turns out that if this property holds for the process under study (in which case it is called ergodic), one can produce useful (i.e., statistically consistent) estimates of the parameters of a process from a single time series.

The autocorrelation function provides a considerable amount of information about the behavior of relatively well behaved (covariance stationary)[5] processes. However, in any realization of a substantively interesting process, the specific elements governing the behavior of the process are empirically confounded among themselves and with a series of "noise" factors. As in many data analysis situations faced by social scientists, there is a need for an analytic device for decomposing the process in terms of some more elementary components and representing the contributions of each to the variance of the overall process. The presence of autocorrelation, however, makes it difficult to achieve this in the temporal domain—where observations are ordered by time of occurrence.

Spectral analysis applies Fourier transformations to the autocovariance or autocorrelation functions to induce a shift to what is called the "frequency domain" (where variation in the process is decomposed in "frequencies"). The derivatives of these transforms (if they exist), called spectral density functions, represent the process in terms of a number of orthogonal components and express the unique contribution of each to the overall variance of the process. That is, this technique enables one to represent mathematically and graphically the separate movements of the elementary components of any empirical instance of a process.

The components are expressed as frequencies or "waves" due to the nature of a Fourier transform. The key properties of each component are its period (length in time units of its cycles or fluctuations) and amplitude

---

[5] A process is said to be covariance stationary if it has finite mean and its autocorrelation function depends only on the time units separating observations, i.e., is independent of historical time.

(magnitude of the swings away from the mean of the process in the course of cycles). Without background in this type of analysis, it is difficult to grasp intuitively the details of a spectral representation. The only important detail for our present purposes is the possibility of decomposition into components which differ in both the amount they contribute to the variance of the process and in their periodicity.

There is one additional aspect of spectral analysis we must mention before discussing the application to aggregation analysis. We noted above that in empirical instances of a process a number of situation-specific features produce "noise" in the series of observations we obtain. Once a spectral representation has been achieved, the analyst usually wishes to eliminate or average out some of the frequencies produced by noise factors (e.g., seasonal fluctuations). The procedure for accomplishing this is called filtering the process. The most usual application of filters is to the smoothing out of erratic fluctuations in the time series.

The notion of filtering brings us back to aggregation problems. Consider the case of aggregation when in a time series of length T, sets of adjacent observations are averaged and the time series recomputed on the averages. This constitutes one type of filter on the process. In particular, this filter averages out the components which have periods less than the interval over which averages are taken.[6] To understand what aggregation does to our parameter estimates, we must be able to specify exactly what frequencies have been eliminated and what substantive interpretation ought to be attached to the components represented in those frequencies. We have made the same point earlier in discussing aggregation relations or grouping criteria.

Quantitative geographers, notably Curry [1966, 1967] and Casetti [1966], have generalized this approach to the areal aggregation problem. Here we translate from a series in a single dimension (time) to one in two dimensions (Euclidian space), i.e., from time series to space series. As Curry [1967, p. 271] points out, a single distance rule makes substantive sense only when the area under investigation is homogeneous in some sense; which point brings us back to the recurring underlying problem in all aggregation analyses— population heterogeneity. (The spectral approach applied mechanically cannot compensate for unanalyzed heterogeneity.) In this case we locate microunits in two dimensions and employ some straightforward rule to calculate distances between them. Autocorrelations are then computed between observations separated by a sequence of fixed distances. That is, the spatial autocorrelation $\rho(d)$ expresses the linear association of states of a spatial process separated by d units of distance.

---

[6] See Curry 1966.

The analysis of aggregation effects proceeds exactly as before. As smaller areal units are consolidated, the components with frequencies with "period" less than the new areal size are filtered out. Casetti demonstrates that the correlation and regression coefficients can be seen to be functions of the parameters of the spectral distribution. Thus we can use the spectral approach to precisely identify the effects of grouping on correlation and regression coefficients. However, the spectral method is much more general than this and extends to a much wider range of possible aggregation problems. It is important to note that a spectral analysis does not alleviate aggregation problems, but provides an alternative method of explicating the effects of groupings on parameter estimates. Very little work on this problem has been reported, however.

Summary

We have seen that in the aggregation problem most familiar to sociologists, the effect of grouping on bivariate product moment correlation coefficients, we can be quite precise in specifying the effects of changing units of analysis. Much of the sociological literature stresses the clustering effect. When areal or temporal units are aggregated, variation in those variables which exhibit clustering tends to be manipulated systematically. Robinson's manipulations of theorems from the analysis of covariance suggests that it would be highly unlikely in such cases for the ecological (or macro) correlation to be equal to the individual (or micro) correlation. It is a well-documented fact that the former tend to be much larger than the latter. Duncan, Cuzzort, and Duncan's elaboration of analysis of covariance results demonstrated that there is a rather complicated relationship between the micro- and aggregate-level correlation and regression coefficients. In particular, they demonstrated that the aggregate-level coefficients are not weighted averages of the grouped individual or microlevel coefficients, but that they depend on the degree of clustering at the microlevel.

Alker's formulation of the covariance theorems illustrates the formal equivalence of spatial and temporal aggregation. Hopefully, this approach will alert social scientists to the previously ignored problems involved in grouping temporally ordered observations.

Blalock has placed the aggregation problem in a more general context and has established the necessity for examining the causal relationships between the aggregation criterion variable (e.g., place of residence, time period, etc.) and the independent variable(s) and dependent variable of concern. We have become increasingly impressed as this analysis has proceeded of the importance of fully specifying the system of causal relations (including the aggregation criterion variable even though it may not be of theoretical or substantive significance) in order to make some judgement on the extent to which variation in each of the variables in the given model has been altered in aggregation. We continue this perspective in the following chapter.

Cramer has proven that when the grouping or aggregation procedure operates on the independent variable, least squares provides an unbiased slope estimate. It is worth noting again that, as Blalock has pointed out, it is crucial to make assumptions about the direction of causal relations before undertaking the analysis since, when variation in X is manipulated, b_{xy} increases in direct proportion to R^2_{xy} while the expected value of b_{yx} remains constant. While aggregating according to X does not bias the slope estimate, it does increase its standard error. Cramer demonstrated further that this increase in the standard error depends both on the number of observations aggregated and the number of aggregate observations formed. It is directly proportional to the number of microobservations making up each aggregate in the general case.

Cramer's results apply directly to the class of aggregation procedures in which variation in the independent variable is directly manipulated. It would be interesting to examine this issue over a wider class of aggregation or grouping procedures. We should be careful not to let Cramer's analysis lull us into thinking that aggregation or grouping of units will not generally bias slope estimates. We noted that when we expand our focus to multivariate recursive models, we see the possibility of a great number of complications. As we have already stressed, we are convinced that resolution of any specific aggregation problem is likely to require the specification of the operative variables "hidden" in the aggregation criterion and of the connections of these factors with the other variables in the model. Alker's rethinking (building on Blalock's analysis) of Robinson's simple model in this sense paves the way for a new approach to the cross-sectional aggergation problem. In the next chapter, we will examine a particular variation of this general approach suggested by Boudon.

The spectral approach to aggregation further emphasizes the formal equivalence of areal and temporal aggregation. This method, while little used to this point, shows promise for specifying a wide variety of aggregation effects.

4

Disaggregation

The demonstration of an aggregation problem defines the disaggregation problem. By now it is clear that grouping microobservations tends to produce changes in correlation and (in special cases) regression coefficients. This development makes it quite obvious that the tendency for large numbers of social scientists to employ available aggregate data in making inferences to microrelationships is ill-advised. In this chapter, we examine the existing approaches (rather those known to this author) to disaggregation, in an attempt to specify the status of knowledge in this problem area.

In our analyses of the aggregation problem, we stressed the need for using a priori information such as theoretical deductions or empirical knowledge for unraveling the complicating effects of grouping in concrete cases. It is clear that problems of disaggregation are more complex than problems of aggregation. Recall that we are requiring that the macrovariables be mathematical transformations of the values of corresponding micro-variables. In the most usual cases, the macrovariables will be sums, means, or proportions. We expect, in the absence of any a priori information, that a given set of such summary statistics can be generated by an almost limitless number of microdistributions. Viewed from this perspective the disaggregation problem becomes one of attempting to employ theoretical propositions, empirical knowledge, and previous research to somehow recover or set limits on the class of microrelations which correspond to the observed macrorelation, given the aggregation relations. The strategies put forward as partial resolutions to the disaggregation problem provide concrete examples of this strategy.

The most dramatic aggregation effects (with the exception of the spurious-ness issue raised by Alker, which has not been treated in earlier disaggregation discussions) involves the inflation of correlation coefficients. For this reason and also because sociologists still do not focus much attention on regression coefficients, the available disaggregation strategies deal with inferences from "ecological" data to microcorrelations.

It will help to set the stage for what follows to recall that Robinson categorically condemned *all* attempts at disaggregating aggregate correlation coefficients. The earliest responses to his position attempted to demonstrate that he had overstated his case and to suggest strategies that would allow valid inference to individual correlations from aggregate data in special cases. From our perspective, the most interesting development in addressing this problem was Goodman's use of the assumptions underlying the linear model. As Boudon clearly points out, the linear model in this context constitutes an implicit theory and disaggregation is successful when the theory is appropriate. Boudon goes on to suggest a nonlinear extension of this general strategy. We will consider these developments in some detail below.

The Method of Bounds

The first-suggested modification of Robinson's blanket rejection of dis-aggregation was the suggestion by Duncan and Davis [1953] that if one cannot correctly infer the exact value of an individual correlation from aggregate data, at least one can set bounds on the value of this statistic.[1] They applied principles developed by Yule and Kendall [1950] for drawing inferences from incomplete data and testing the consistency of data to this problem. The suggested procedure involves a systematic examination of the marginal totals for each region employed in the ecological analysis. Duncan and Davis confined their attention to the cross-classification of dichotomies (two-by-two tables). It is well known that a single-cell value together with the marginal totals completely specifies all of the cell values in a two-by-two table. The microcorrelation is computed in this case using the internal cell frequencies, while the ecological (between-group) correlation employs only the marginal values. Duncan and Davis employed as a substantive example the cross-classification of race and occupational status (domestic, non-domestic) for women in Chicago. Table 4–1, which gives the marginal values for the first subregion (census tract in this instance), is typical of the data available in an ecological analysis. In this case, Duncan and Davis focused on the top left cell. At a minimum there are no white women in domestic employment in this census tract. At a maximum, there are 95 (and thus, in this case, 144) nonwhite women. The microcorrelation is then computed using first the maximum value in this cell (and the corresponding values produced in the other cells) and then the minimum value. This technique is successively applied to each subarea. In the substantive example, the

---

[1] There is a brief literature in geography on this issue, which will not be considered here. A. H. Robinson [1956] suggested a rather mechanical weighting of values which would make correlation and regression coefficients invariant under aggregation. His approach was criticized by Thomas and Anderson [1965]. Both the original suggestion and the criticism seem to miss the point of the clustering effect and therefore are largely irrelevant if not misleading.

individual correlation was .289. This method of setting bounds used on each of the 935 census tracts produced bounds of .126 and .355.

Table 4–1. A Race–Employment Example of the Disaggregation Problem

	Domestic	Nondomestic	
White			95
Nonwhite			782
	239	638	

These authors note that different areal divisions produce different bounds and suggest that the logic of the procedure dictates that the least minimum and greatest maximum among the results from alternative areal divisions be employed. They note further that the range of possibilities produced by this procedure do not constitute a set of confidence limits in the probabilistic sense, but rather "provide absolute upper and lower bounds for their [true cell frequencies and correlation] values." This last remark is not intended as a qualification of the strategy. On the contrary, this is a strong statement and implies that one can be absolutely certain that the individual correlation lies within the bounds arrived at. If these were a set of probabilistic confidence limits, we would only have certainty that the procedure would produce bounds containing the desired parameter a given (by the probability level selected) proportion of the time "in the long run." On the other hand, this procedure is limited by the necessity of obtaining areal marginals on enough units so that the limits are not so wide as to convey almost no information. Duncan and Davis point out that their strategy is much more successful when finer areal subdivisions (census tracts rather than districts) are employed. Nonetheless, this does seem a valuable approach in some kinds of exploratory research. For some reason, it does not seem to have been used in published research.

Goodman [1959] has systematized and extended this somewhat intuitive method of obtaining bounds. He began by examining the assertion that finer subdivisions tend to produce narrower bounds with such data. Goodman suggested that there may be some subdivisions which do not differ from other levels of aggregation in the bounds obtained. That is, some subareas can be combined without changing the bounds. Tracts that can be combined in such a way he calls "similar."

Thus the fact that substantially closer bounds were obtained when census tracts rather than community areas were used indicates that some of the tracts that form a given community area were not "similar." [1959, p. 617]

Goodman then developed a method of combining areas so that the same bounds are obtained for the combined areas as for the finer subdivisions. He began by drawing two lines $Y = X$ and $Y = 1 - X$ (where X and Y are proportions) on the scattergram of the observed ecological variables Y and X. This divides the graph into four parts: A, B, C, and D, where A contains all those points representing areas in which the number of nonwhite employed females (using Duncan and Davis' example) was not more than the number of females in domestic service and the number of females in domestic service was not more than the number of white employed females $(X \leq Y \leq 1 - X)$; B contains those points where $X \geq Y \leq 1 - X$; C contains those points where $X \geq Y \geq 1 - X$; and D those points where $X \leq Y \geq 1 - X$. Any point falling on one of the dividing lines can be assigned arbitrarily to one of the adjacent areas. An important result is that weighted (by relative population size) averages of the values X and Y are taken from each of the areas represented in each of the regions of the scatter-diagram by a point, the bounds obtained using these four weighted averages will be equal to the bounds obtained using the information on all of the areas in the study. Or, in terms of the presentation on the preceding page, this partition of the scatterplot divides the ecological areas into four *similarity groups*.

The reasoning behind this statement is not exactly obvious and is not clearly presented in Goodman's paper. We will attempt briefly to suggest why this statement is true. We think it will be helpful to confine our attention to a single region of the scatterplot, say A. We can see, first of all, that the minimum individual correlation for all units falling in this region is exactly zero. This is seen by noting that the proportion of the female labor force in domestic employment (Y) is less than or equal to the proportion of the female labor force that is white $(1 - X)$. Even in the limiting case in which these two proportions are equal for all of the units in A, it is conceivable that every employed female in domestic service is white. Similarly it can be seen that the maximum possible individual correlation for each unit depends solely on the number of nonwhite females in the labor force in each area. That is, the maximum possible number of nonwhite females in domestic employment is the number of employed nonwhite females since, Y—the proportion of the female labor force engaged in domestic employment—is greater than or equal to the proportion of the female labor force that is nonwhite. Thus it is possible that every employed nonwhite female in these areas is a domestic.

It is easy to see in the case of the minimum possible individual correlation than an average of X and Y values for the units in A will produce the same estimate of the minimal correlation as will be obtained using each unit separately. Every unit contributing to the average has exactly the same minimum value, which is zero. In the second case, the maximum correlation, the estimate for each unit depends only on a single value. Thus, an average of these unit values that has been standardized by relative population size will produce a value for the number of nonwhite females employed as domestics which includes exactly the same information as the set of all the individual areal units falling in A. Thus the same upper bound will be obtained.

Goodman demonstrates further that one can immediately judge the accuracy of the bounds obtained by examining the degree to which the summary points (the weighted averages) "hug" the four sides of the graph. In the special case, where all of the ecological areas can be represented by summary points that lie on the boundaries of the graph, the ecological correlation is exactly equal to the individual correlation. The derivation of these results will not be presented here in the interest of brevity, since they are contained in the paper cited and would require rather extensive exposition.

Application of a Linear Model

Goodman's analysis of the method of bounds was somewhat incidental to his main task, which was to propose another method through which, "In *very special circumstances* the study of the regression between ecological variables may be used to make inferences concerning the behavior of individuals" [1959, p. 663]. He notes that sociologists study the regression between ecological variables because they are interested in the questions this kind of study can answer (e.g., many aspects of demography and ecology).

Another reason why sociologists study the regression between ecological variables is that they think that such a study may be used to make inferences concerning the behavior of individuals. In one sense these sociologists are incorrect and in another sense they are quite correct . . . knowledge of the ecological correlations cannot *in general* be used to make inferences concerning individual behavior. Since, however, sociologists continue to use ecological correlations to make such inferences, it is of interest to see in what circumstances these inferences are justified. [Goodman 1959, p. 663]

Goodman continued the race–literacy example in presenting his argument. The development will be easier to grasp if we begin by considering the fourfold table illustrated in Table 4-2.

Table 4–2. Linear Model for the Race–Literacy Disaggregation Problem

		Literacy		
		Literate	Illiterate	
Race	White	a	b	$a + b$
	Nonwhite	c	d	$c + d$
		$a + c$	$b + d$	N

Goodman defines the following terms:

$Y = (b + d)/N$ is the proportion of the population which is illiterate

$X = (c + d)/N$ is the proportion nonwhite

$p = d/(c + d)$ is the proportion of nonwhites who are illiterate

$r = b/(a + b)$ is the proportion of whites who are illiterate

The problem as it has been developed to this point has been to estimate or set limits on p and r given a knowledge of X and Y. Goodman shows that the proportion of the population who are illiterate, Y, can be written as

$$Y = Xp + (1 - X)r$$

This is a simple algebraic identity, given the definitions above. The reader can convince himself of this by substituting these identities into this expression and simplifying. By a further manipulation we obtain

$$Y = r + (p - r)X$$

This expression is in the form of a bivariate linear relationship, $Y = a + bX$. If the proportions p and r are constant across all of the regions or sub-populations being studied (these proportions do not vary from region to region), then there will be an exact (deterministic) relationship between X and Y for the different regions. A straight line fitted to the observed data points (values of X and Y) could be used to determine $r = a$ and $p = b + a$. That is, in this very special case, we can use examination of a simple linear model to obtain the missing information needed to determine the individual correlation.

We can relate this point to the analysis in Chapter 3. If there is no variation in r and p across regions, the two correlation ratios, E_{XR}^2 and E_{YR}^2, are zero. In verbal terms, the area-grouping criterion does not account for any of the variation in either X or Y. The situation, then, corresponds to the limiting case of expression (3.11) noted by Robinson, where the individual correlation R_{XY} is exactly equal to the within-region correlation WR_{XY}. Examination of expression (3.10) shows that, in this case, the between-aggregate or "ecological correlation" ER_{XY} is equal to zero.

Goodman notes that in actual research it would be extremely unusual for the proportions r and p to be invariant across areas (or time periods). However, the procedures of regression analysis can still be applied if the *conditional expectation* of p for a given value of X, $E(p \mid X)$, and $E(r \mid X)$ are constant for all X values.[2] This condition is the stochastic analogue of the condition just discussed for the deterministic case. If this condition holds, we have:

$$E(Y \mid X) = E(r \mid X) + [E(p \mid X) - E(r \mid X)]X$$

Goodman suggests several checks for the tenability of the assumption that the above identity is applicable to the given empirical situation. First, the method is obviously not recommended when the p and r values vary widely in the different regions (or time periods). If it appears that the assumption can be met for only a subsample of the ecological areas (and by our extention, of time periods), Goodman suggests that only the regions in such a subsample be used in the analysis. A second caution to the application of regression analysis is that the scatterdiagram of the relationship between X and Y should appear to be linear. A third check is that the obtained values of r and p should be in the interval $(0, 1)$ since these quantities are proportions. (Boudon [1963] presented an example in which this condition is not met; the microrelation in this case was nonlinear.) In addition, the estimated proportion of illiterates in the total population $\hat{Y} = \hat{a} + \hat{b}X$ should be close to the known proportion Y. This however, is not an independent check when either proportion, X or Y, is equal to the average proportion for the ecological areas.

When all of these conditions obtain, one can apply the procedures of ordinary least squares with some confidence. Goodman demonstrates that under these conditions, $\hat{b}$ and $\hat{a}$ are unbiased estimates of the population parameters. In the special case where the conditional variance of Y given X, $\sigma^2_{Y|X}$, does not depend on X (homoscedasticity), they are best linear unbiased estimators.[3] However, the only assumption necessary for the

---

[2] In the context of probability theory we define independence of random variables in precisely this way. A random variable X is said to be *independent* of a random variable Y if and only if $E(X \mid Y) = E(X)$ for all values of X and Y. We say that X does not depend on Y.

[3] One of a set of estimators is said to be "best" if it has the smallest variance of all estimators of the same type (e.g., linear).

application of regression techniques is that mentioned above:

$$E(r \mid X) = E(r) \quad \text{and} \quad E(p \mid X) = E(p)$$

This condition necessarily precludes any systematic (or causal) connection between X and either p or r. Shively [1969] demonstrates that Goodman's restrictions are formally equivalent to requiring aggregation only by independent variables.

Goodman applied the above strategy to the race–literacy example originally used by Robinson. In this example, the individual correlation was .20 and the ecological correlation computed on census district totals was .95. The Duncan and Davis bounds were −.07 and .60. This procedure yields an estimate of .38. Applied to the race–employment data used by Duncan and Davis, where the individual correlation was .29 and the bounds were .126 and .355, this yields an estimate of .25.

In suggesting a number of extensions of this procedure to more complicated analysis situations (e.g., 2-by-K cross-classifications, interrelationship of two or more quantitative variables, etc.), Goodman raised an issue which highlights the parallels between his analysis and the discussion in the previous chapter. He first considers the case where the simple linear model is not appropriate; one might adopt a multilinear model of the form

$$E(Y \mid X, Z) = A + BX + CZ$$

where Z is "some relevant variable" and A, B, and C are constant for all regions. Goodman illustrates that in this case one may apply the standard methods of multiple regression analysis to the regional means $\overline{Y}(i)$, $\overline{X}(i)$, and $\overline{Z}(i)$ (where i refers to the region: $i = 1, \ldots, R$) to obtain estimates of the constants A, B, and C in the model formulated at the individual level. But, in the more usual case, Z is a constant for all individuals in a given region. That is, Z is some characteristic of the region (or, more abstractly, of the grouping criterion) such as level of industrialization.

With this variation, the problem now formally corresponds to an analysis of covariance with the regional characteristic taken as the covariable:

$$E(Y \mid X, Z) = (A + CZ) + BZ$$

where the intercept $A + CZ$ may vary from region to region. The thrust of Goodman's argument is that disaggregation inferences may legitimately be made in such a situation if and only if the regional covariable does not interact with the relationship of interest, i.e., the slope is a constant across regions.

We know from Blalock's analysis that the slopes will be biased by the grouping process if variation in the dependent variable is manipulated.

Clearly, Goodman's disaggregation procedure is not appropriate in such situations (which include Alker's example of spurious relations at the aggregate level). So we see that disaggregation may not be overly problematic if we can assure ourselves that only independent variables were manipulated in the grouping process. Of course, in more complicated models, the effects of distinct independent variables may easily become confounded in such a grouping process.

Nonadditive Models

Boudon [1963] argues forcefully that, for theoretical and substantive reasons, linear models are inappropriate for many disaggregation problems. We will consider his objections and proposed alternatives in some detail since they represent a major departure from the broad stream of analyses in this area. He begins with three empirical generalizations which emerged from the examination of a large number of "collective correlations"; they are generally very high, they increase regularly with grouping, and they are generally curvilinear. The first two observations are fully supported in the literature already reported. But the third is a new one; and, unfortunately, Boudon does not offer any evidence in support of his observation. He does, however, employ as examples two pieces of previously published research which do not appear to fit the assumptions of the linear model.

Boudon begins the argument by agreeing that microcorrelations cannot be deduced from aggregate or macrocorrelations. And he correctly points out that if we are unwilling to make any a priori assumptions, the Duncan and Davis method of bounds extracts all of the information possible about the individual correlation. The obvious alternative is to begin making assumptions about the distributions of variables to aid in making disaggregation inferences. The first steps in this process have been taken by Goodman who employed the assumption of linear-additive effects.

Boudon exhibits a useful concern with the substantive implications of what might seem at first glance to be purely technical assumptions. The assumption of linear-additive regional effects is a case in point. In order to illustrate the import of the distinction between additive and nonadditive aggregation models, he employs the following illustrative propositions:

A. Average living space per capita increases with per capita incomes in the districts of Paris.
B. The wealthy sections of Paris vote more conservatively.

He contends that proposition A is simply a substitute for a proposition linking individual income and living conditions but that proposition B is not simply related to a proposition of the form: rich persons tend to vote more conservatively. One might find, for instance, that the poorer residents of wealthy neighborhoods vote more conservatively than the wealthy residents. Thus, Boudon claims that proposition A is reducible to an individual level proposition, but that B is not. His argument, further, is that these two propositions are representative of two types of propositions which embody different assumptions about the influence of the environment. It will follow from this, as we shall see, that the two kinds of propositions are also separated by mathematical considerations.

Unfortunately, Boudon chose to make this crucial distinction illustratively rather than analytically. On first reading, the distinction seems intuitively pleasing and, in the context of his argument, useful. On closer scrutiny, the distinction breaks down, at least to an extent. Consider proposition A. It is certainly possible that within any given geographic area wealthy persons will sacrifice floor space for status and reside in high-status areas with less roomy houses than they could afford in other, lower-status areas. I would not want to push this counter-example too far but it does seem to point to a problem in Boudon's distinction.

It is useful to reformulate the argument in an attempt to make an analytical distinction. We are faced with two observed macrolevel relationships (we can represent as simple causal propositions):

    A. wealth $\rightarrow$ housing
    B. wealth $\rightarrow$ voting behavior

The issue is, on what grounds can we make an analytical distinction between these two propositions (which Boudon indicates represent two classes of propositions). It is helpful to recall that Goodman demonstrated that disaggregation is not problematic if the microrelations do not vary from region to region in the population under study. It appears that Boudon chose proposition A to represent the macroanalogue of this type of microrelation. Proposition B, then, presumably represents the macroanalogue of a microrelation which would tend to exhibit considerable variability across regions (and, by extension, other kinds of groupings). The issue can now be seen to involve in a central way the variance–invariance of the underlying micromodels.

An important consideration is the argument that the two classes of propositions differ markedly in terms of potential environmental influence. It is obvious that Boudon equates variation across groupings as the impact of environment. We must ask, then, why is proposition A likely to be invariant across groupings while B is not. The only abstract formulation we can attempt focuses on the complexity of the underlying bivariate micromodels. Suppose for the sake of argument that there is a strong "universal" direct causal connection between wealth and housing status while wealth and voting behavior are connected in terms of a more complex model (in the population under study). We illustrate this difference in Figure 4-1, where the intervening variables in model B (X, Y, Z) are not specified.

The two models drawn in Figure 4-1 differ in the following important way. Wealth can be seen to be related to housing status in a simple direct way (perhaps this is a "unitary causal process") while the relationship of wealth to voting behavior occurs through a number of (possibly complex) processes. The distinction is useful only when the component processes of this complex process are likely to differ in different groupings (or regions). More specifically, we can see that in a model like model B the values of the intervening variables X, Y, and Z, their interrelations, and their relations with other

Figure 4-1. Boudon's Two Types of Propositions Illustrated.

variables both included and excluded from the model are likely to be affected by grouping procedures. In other words, they are likely to be subject to environmental influences (when the grouping is defined regionally and where the regions have some meaningful identity).

This reformulation also faces considerable difficulties, however. As the reader has undoubtedly noted, almost any bivariate causal relationship can be further specified by the introduction of additional intervening variables. Nevertheless, it appears to make sense to begin to distinguish between relationships on the basis of the degree to which it is probable that complex intervening processes are operating and the likelihood that such processes are influenced by variations in grouping (e.g., environmental) properties. Unfortunately, such distinctions would demand considerable subtlety of theoretical development and substantive knowledge; and the discussion at the present time is entirely heuristic. The only claim we make is that this seems a reasonable direction in which to formulate the distinction Boudon employs in attempting to address environmental effects. Hopefully the import of this distinction will become salient as we proceed with the exposition of Boudon's analysis.

Now let us turn to the substantive implications of linear-additive vs. nonadditive formulations. We have already seen that when the linear model fits (i.e., when there is no areal or environmental effect or when such an effect is additive) Goodman's technique produces fairly good estimates of micro-level coefficients. Boudon asserts that the linear model in this context constitutes a veritable theory which is both formal and sociological. Consider proposition B above. A linear model as a formal model rests on the following axiom: the propensity of wealthy people to vote conservative is a constant across all ecological areas. In particular, this propensity does not depend on either the number of wealthy people in the area or on the number of conservative votes. Boudon points out that the regression model exactly specifies the formulation of this axiom. He also points out that the formal model rests on a sociological postulate of a form like the following: the propensity of rich people to vote conservatively does not depend on the environment of the electoral district. A wealthy man in a high-status area has the same propensity as a wealthy man living in a working-class area.

Thus, Boudon identifies the linear model as the limiting case and because of the restrictiveness of the underlying sociological postulate, concludes that the linear model is not suitable for most substantively interesting investigations involving disaggregation. He states this position in strong terms and overstates the case against the use of linear models. In addition, it appears that he takes an extremely narrow view of what is substantively interesting. Since he argues that propositions like A fit the disaggregation requirements of the linear model, he seems to reject as interesting those relationships where bivariate relations seem to suffice. Regardless, his main point is well taken. There are a wide variety of disaggregation situations of potential interest to sociologists in which linear-model techniques are not suitable.

Perhaps the most important contribution of Boudon's paper is to suggest an approach to disaggregation in cases in which the aggregation criterion interacts with the relationship of interest, i.e., in nonadditive cases. This strategy is developed for disaggregating relations among dichotomous variables (proportions). We have seen that Goodman's linear technique for estimating the microparameters p and q depends on the estimation of another series of parameters, i.e., the intercept and slope of the regression function defined on the aggregate observations. The second step in the process is the deduction of the microparameters p and q from the least squares estimates a and b. Boudon points out that it is possible to estimate the regression coefficients and not have enough information by which to deduce the second set of parameters from the first. In other words, it is possible to have different parameter estimates corresponding with a single set of regression parameters. We have seen that the restrictions of linearity and additivity allow one to correctly deduce p and q from a and b.

Boudon has developed a technique of using theoretical assumptions or empirical knowledge to make possible the deduction of the microparameters in nonadditive cases in the same way that the assumptions of linearity and additivity make possible the deduction of p and q in Goodman's procedure. Perhaps an example will help here. Boudon considers two nonadditive models. In the first, we assume that the individual propensities p and q depend on the *frequency* of the dependent variable (i.e., of a certain behavior) in the environment. In this case, we let both p and q be functions of Y, the dependent variable. The second model assumes that the individual propensities depend on the *composition* of the environment. Boudon's example is that it is likely that poor workers will have a higher propensity to vote communist in working-class neighborhoods than in higher-status neighborhoods. In this case, we let both p and q (now defined as propensities of workers and entrepreneurs, respectively, to vote communist) be functions of X (the proportion of the population in the district working class). The resulting model would then have

$$p = a_1 X + b_1 \quad \text{and} \quad q = a_2 X + b_2$$

and the regression becomes

$$Y = (a_1 - a_2)X^2 + (b_1 - b_2 + a_2)X + b_2$$

This, then, is a parabolic regression curve. We can use techniques of non-linear regression to estimate the parameters A, B, and C of the regression function

$$Y = AX^2 + BX + C$$

However, we have four unknowns, a_1, a_2, b_1, and b_2, so we cannot deduce these from A, B, and C without further restrictions on the model. As Boudon puts it, we must introduce supplementary hypotheses. He suggests some possible supplementary hypotheses for this model. We might assume (or know from previous research) that $a_2 = 0$, i.e., that the propensity of non-workers to vote communist does not depend on the composition (defined in the narrow sense of proportion of the district working class) of the district. Or we might assume that $b_2 = 0$, i.e., that the propensity of nonworkers to vote communist would be null when there are no working men in the district. Finally, we might desire for reasons of logical structure that the propensity of workers to vote communist be null when the proportion of workers in the district is zero. In this case, we would set $b_1 = 0$. Any one of these restrictions make possible the deduction of the remaining micropropensities from the regression estimates.

Boudon employed data from Belgian elections to estimate the coefficients of the parabolic regression in which he assumed $b_1 = 0$ (the last supplementary hypothesis discussed above).[4] The formal model was, then,

$$Y = (a_1 - a_2)X^2 + (a_2 - b_2)X + b_2$$

The estimated coefficients of the parabola were

$$Y = 2.2X^2 - .4X + .2$$

Thus the estimate of a_1 is 1.8, of a_2 is $-.6$, and of b_2 is .2.

The final step in Boudon's strategy is to examine the substantive implications of the estimated micropropensities. In this case, since the estimated value of a_2 is $-.6$, the model suggests that the propensity of nonworkers to vote communist is a decreasing linear function of the proportion of the population in the district who are workers. This, of course, can be verified empirically. Boudon suggests that this conclusion is unlikely to be supported, in which case the model is rejected. The process continues until the analyst finds a model which is both theoretically pleasing and whose deduced estimates survive empirical verification. If such a model is found, then the micro- or individual correlation can be computed from the estimated individual propensities. Finally, as Goodman extended his procedure to quantitative variables, this procedure may also be extended.

Thus, if we are willing or able to make a series of theoretical assumptions about a model, it is possible to deduce the individual or microlevel coefficients from aggregated data. Of course, the results depend on the adequacy of the assumptions made; the better the state of knowledge in any given area, the easier it is to disaggregate. This is somewhat unfortunate since it is precisely in areas in which we have the least coherent knowledge that we are likely to attempt disaggregation. If we had adequate microlevel propositions and could test them with appropriate microdata, there would be little need for disaggregation.

As we have mentioned previously, this explicit example of the use of theoretical, "logical," and empirical knowledge and assumptions serves as a model for the aggregation strategy advocated here. Boudon clearly illustrates the manner in which the use of such a priori information can set limits to the aggregation–disaggregation problem and allow the testing of explicit models

---

[4] It is these data which were referred to earlier. In estimating the microcoefficients with these data, Boudon obtained an estimate for the quantity $(p - q)$ to be greater than unity which is a "logical contradiction" since this quantity is supposed to represent a difference of proportions. For this reason, he rejects the linear model and used a parabolic model.

in the face of such problems. Without belaboring the point, it would seem that the whole status of our knowledge of the aggregation–disaggregation problem would be considerably enhanced by a series of examinations in the spirit of those presented by Boudon.

Summary

We opened this chapter by suggesting that the results on aggregation would suggest that disaggregation would be a very hazardous research technique. However, several social scientists have reacted to W. S. Robinson's blanket condemnation of attempts to disaggregate. Duncan and Davis have demonstrated that if the analyst has access to data on a number of ecological subareas, he can employ the "method of bounds" without any assumptions about the aggregating procedure to set absolute limits on the individual level correlation. We have seen that these limits tend to be rather wide in practice, communicating relatively little information about the microlevel correlation. Also, the extension of the method of bounds beyond the cross-classification of dichotomous variables has not been demonstrated. Yet, as Boudon has pointed out, this technique extracts all of the information possible about the microcorrelation when no assumptions are made about the relations between the aggregation criterion variable and the independent and dependent variables of interest. Goodman demonstrated that if the assumption of linear-additive relation between aggregation criteria variables and the relationship of interest can be justified, one can make inferences from aggregated data to microcorrelation and regression coefficients using regression analysis. Boudon has criticized the linear regression approach on the grounds of limited substantive interest and has advocated the use of models in which the aggregating criterion (he restricts himself to areal aggregation) interacts with the relationship of interest. He demonstrated that the estimation models appropriate in such situations are likely to be nonlinear regression models and has developed an explicit strategy for employing existing empirical knowledge together with logical statements and theoretical assumptions for deriving individual-level coefficients from the estimated parameters of a number of nonlinear models. Finally, in discussing Boudon's analysis we suggested that previous analyses may have implicitly used a distinction between classes of propositions (with distinct relationships with environmental variables). It is difficult to formalize this distinction. We finally arrived at the position that the key to this difficulty is the complexity of the underlying bivariate micromodels. Bivariate microrelations which are "universal" are, by definition, not subject to environmental influence of any sort. As one moves from this pole towards the situation in which pairs of variables are related through very complex causal processes, we see that the probability of major environmental influences is greatly increased. This occurs as the values of the intervening variables (and, in extreme cases, even the form of the relations) depends on the value of grouping or regional properties. The practical utility of this formulation of the implicit distinction has yet to be demonstrated, however.

5 Aggregation in Static Models Estimated from Panel Data

The bulk of sociological research has employed static models estimated at a single point in time. Economists, on the other hand, have generally used serial observations in estimating their models. Thus, the economically oriented analyses of the aggregation problem tend to consider the general case of K-variable models which are estimated from a temporal series of observations. Not surprisingly, these analyses appear quite different from those presented in Chapter 3. We will see, however, that a causal perspective on the aggregation problem reveals important points of convergence of the two approaches.

We must distinguish here between a static model estimated from a time-series and a dynamic model. In the latter case, the temporal dimension enters explicitly into the model, but this is not true of the case we are considering. The analysis which follows has been extended to apply to the simplest type of dynamic models, models which employ lagged endogenous variables.[1]

There are several trends in contemporary sociology which suggest that the use of time-series observations will greatly increase in the near future. One of the more important trends is the adoption from demography of the cohort model for the study of patterns of mobility, of educational achievement, and like phenomena.[2] There are an increasing number of studies in progress which have obtained baseline measures on some cohort of interest, e.g., freshman in a particular high school, with the intention of following up the cohort and remeasuring such variables at fixed time intervals, e.g., one year after graduation and at five-year intervals after that. Perhaps more frequent at the present time is the use of "synthetic cohorts" where measures at previous specified time periods are obtained retrospectively from a presently defined cohort.[3] Similar trends are obvious in the more macroquantitative comparative studies of social change, evolution, and societal development. As such studies rely increasingly on quantitative indicators, e.g., per capita income, kilowatt consumption of electricity per capita, literacy rates, etc., the data and models employed will tend to more closely approximate those

---

[1] For a discussion of this extension, see Theil [1954].

[2] See Ryder [1965].

[3] See Blau and Duncan [1967].

now used by economists. Such time-series estimates would seem essential in any study of social change or evolution.

Theil's Formulation

We turn our attention to Theil's [1954] immensely important formulation of the aggregation problem.[4] As before, we restrict ourselves to linear aggregation. Consider the following *micromodel*:

$$y_i(t) = \alpha_i + \sum_{k=1}^{K} \beta_{ki} x_{ki}(t) + u_i(t) \qquad i = 1, \dots, N \qquad (5.1)$$

where each microunit is permitted to behave idiosyncratically with respect to changes in the K microexplanatory variables; the t in parentheses denotes the time period of the observation; and the disturbances are assumed to have zero mean. For the moment, we will consider the simplest case of aggregation in which all macrovariables are the sums of the values of corresponding microvariables (the extension to arithmetic means and proportions is trivial).

$$y(t) = \sum_{i=1}^{N} y_i(t)$$

$$x_1(t) = \sum_{i=1}^{N} x_{1i}(t) \qquad (5.2)$$

$$\vdots$$

$$x_K(t) = \sum_{i=1}^{N} x_{Ki}(t)$$

We assume that a *macromodel* is defined analogous to equation (5.1):

$$y(t) = \alpha + \sum_{k=1}^{K} \beta_k x_k(t) + u(t) \qquad (5.3)$$

The analytic problem arises when we use least squares to estimate the macromodel directly, and compare the obtained coefficients with those obtained in estimating the micromodel. The notion of simple consistency would suggest that we would want the macrocoefficients to be simple sums of the corresponding microcoefficients. We can use our formulation of the consistency requirement to see this. Consistency is achieved when two methods

---

[4] Excellent summary statements of Theil's analysis have been prepared for economists by Allen [1956, ch. 20] and Fox [1968, ch. 14]. Our notation follows Allen.

of generating predicted macrovalues for the dependent variable are identical. We can express changes in the macromodel as follows:

$$\Delta y(t) = \alpha + \sum_{k=1}^{K} \beta_k \, \Delta x_k(t) + \Delta u(t) \qquad (5.4)$$

For each equation in the micromodel (where we allow each microunit to be represented by a separate equation), change is defined as

$$\Delta y_i(t) = \alpha_i + \sum_{k=1}^{K} \beta_{ki} \, \Delta x_{ki}(t) + \Delta u_i(t) \qquad (5.5)$$

Consistency, then, requires that

$$\Delta y(t) = \sum_{i=1}^{N} \Delta y_i(t) = \sum_{i=1}^{N} \alpha_i + \sum_{i=1}^{N} \sum_{k=1}^{K} \beta_{ki} \, \Delta x_{ki}(t) + \sum_{i=1}^{N} \Delta u_i(t) \quad (5.6)$$

In other words, when the aggregates are simple sums, aggregation is consistent, if and only if

$$\alpha = \sum_{i=1}^{N} \alpha_i, \qquad \beta_k = \sum_{i=1}^{N} \beta_{ki}, \qquad u(t) = \sum_{i=1}^{N} u_i(t) \qquad (5.7)$$

There is nothing obscure in these definitions of the macrocoefficients. This result agrees with intuition. We can see that substitution of the values defined in (5.7) into the original macromodel equation (5.3) will yield equation (5.6) as required.

Theil's contribution is in large measure a concise demonstration and proof that one will generally not be so fortunate as to obtain the required macro-coefficients even when all relations are linear. To pursue this and the resulting contradictions between micro- and macromodels we need to define a new set of functions. We define a set of *auxiliary regressions* which express each microvariable as a linear function of the whole set of macrovariables. More precisely, they are the least squares estimates of the "time paths" of changes in the microvariables as functions of changes in the macrovariables.

$$x_{ki}(t) = A_{ki} + B_{ki,1} x_1(t) + \cdots + B_{ki,K} x_K(t) + V_{ki}(t) \qquad (5.8)$$

where $V_{ki}(t)$ are residuals which are assumed to have zero mean and to be uncorrelated with the macrovariables. We need not assign any substantive meaning to these auxiliary regressions since they are simply a set of formal relationships which we use in establishing the likely presence of aggregation bias. We will see below, however, that it is helpful to carefully analyze the relationships between microvariables and noncorresponding macrovariables in addressing any aggregation problem in which a time-series of observations is employed.

Theil's Theorem 1 demonstrates that the parameters of equation (5.3), the macromodel, are determined as follows (when the aggregates are simple sums):

$$\alpha = \sum_{i=1}^{N} \alpha_i + \sum_{k=1}^{K} \sum_{i=1}^{N} A_{ki}\beta_{ki}$$

$$\beta_k = \sum_{k'=1}^{K} \sum_{i=1}^{N} B_{k'i,k}\beta_{k'i} \qquad k = 1, \ldots, K \qquad (5.9)$$

$$u(t) = \sum_{i=1}^{N} u_i(t) + \sum_{i=1}^{N} \sum_{k=1}^{K} \beta_{ki}V_{ki}(t)$$

Thus the macroparameter estimates have some rather unusual properties:

1. The macrointercept is the sum of the corresponding microcoefficients plus a series of terms involving noncorresponding parameters.
2. The macroregression coefficients, which can be rewritten as

$$\beta_k = \sum_{i=1}^{N} \beta_{ki} + \sum_{i=1}^{N} \left(B_{ki,k} - \frac{1}{N}\right)\beta_{ki} + \sum_{i=1}^{N} \sum_{k' \neq k} B_{k'i,k}\beta_{k'i} \qquad (5.10)$$

are the arithmetic means of the corresponding microcoefficients β_{ki}, plus weighted arithmetic means of the corresponding microcoefficients β_{ki}, plus weighted arithmetic means of noncorresponding microcoefficients $\beta_{k'i}$.
3. The macrodisturbance is composed of a sum of corresponding micro-values plus a weighted sum of noncorresponding coefficients.

It is the presence of the terms involving noncorresponding parameters (Allen calls these "cross-effects") which is disturbing. Theil labels all terms other than

$$\sum_{i=1}^{N} \alpha_i, \qquad \frac{1}{N}\sum_{i=1}^{N} \beta_{ki} \text{ (or } \bar{\beta}_{ki}), \qquad \sum_{i=1}^{N} u_i(t) \qquad (5.11)$$

as *aggregation bias terms*.

We can further analyze these bias terms by employing the second half of Theil's Theorem 1 which states that the following restrictions on the coefficients of the auxiliary regressions must hold.

$$\sum_{i=1}^{N} A_{ki} = \sum_{i=1}^{N} V_{ki}(t) = 0, \qquad \sum_{i=1}^{N} B_{k'i,k} = \begin{cases} 1 \text{ if } k' = k \\ 0 \text{ otherwise} \end{cases} \qquad (5.12)$$

We want this requirement to be met since we have defined

$$x_k = \sum_{i=1}^{N} x_{ki}$$

and the summation of expression (5.8) will not yield this result unless these restrictions are met. Using these restrictions we can rewrite the expressions of (5.9) so as to represent the bias terms as covariances between microparameters and coefficients of the auxiliary regression. For example,

$$\sum_{i=1}^{N} (A_{ki} - \bar{A}_k)(\beta_{ki} - \bar{\beta}_k) = \sum_{i=1}^{N} (\beta_{ki} - \bar{\beta}_k)A_{ki} = \sum_{i=1}^{N} \beta_{ki}A_{ki}$$

since, by (5.12),[5]

$$\sum_{i=1}^{N} A_{ki} = 0 \qquad (\bar{A}_k \text{ and } \bar{\beta}_k \text{ are arithmetic means})$$

Hence we have

$$\alpha = \sum_{i=1}^{N} \alpha_i + N \sum_{k=1}^{K} \text{cov}(A_{ki}, \beta_{ki})$$

$$\beta_k = \bar{\beta}_{ki} + N \sum_{k'=1}^{K} \text{cov}(B_{k'i,k}, \beta_{ki}) \qquad (5.13)$$

$$u(t) = \sum_{i=1}^{N} u_i(t) + N \sum_{k=1}^{K} \text{cov}[V_{ki}(t), \beta_{ki}]$$

Thus, we see that the three macroterms (two coefficients and the disturbance term) are all equal to linear combinations of the corresponding microterms apart from certain covariance corrections. *These covariance corrections represent the aggregation bias in the estimated macromodel.* In other words, it is the presence of such covariance terms which give rise to inconsistencies between analogous models estimated at different levels of aggregation (given, of course, that the micro- and macrovariables are functionally related). The reader may convince himself of this by reexamining the two-stage prediction procedure outlined above in the development of the notion of consistency.

Consider the suicide-function example developed earlier. We can imagine a situation in which a series of time-series studies involve estimation of the "same" function at, say, three levels of aggregation: the individual level, the census-tract level, and the state level. The census-tract measures would involve an aggregation of individual values and the state levels would involve an aggregation of census-tract values. We can see from equations (5.13) that the three estimated models would be consistent only in the special case in which all aggregation bias terms vanished. Nonzero covariances of non-corresponding micro- and macrovariables insure that the predictions made from the three models will not be consistent. The presence of such covariance

---

[5] This presentation follows Green [1964, ch. 12].

terms in the aggregate parameter estimates cannot be accounted for within a homology framework. Unless additional variables are introduced into the macromodels to account for such aggregation effects, these covariance terms must represent an aggregation complication.

Before addressing the possible sources of such aggregation bias, we will mention three special cases in which such aggregation bias is ruled out.

1. To this point we have allowed the microunits to react idiosyncratically to changes in the explanatory variables of concern as long as all microunits' behavior could be represented by linear functions (i.e., we allowed the regression parameters to vary). We see in (5.13) that each of the covariance corrections involves the microparameters. We know that the covariance of a constant with any random variable is zero. Thus, if the microparameters are constants, there can be no aggregation bias. The economists who have addressed the aggregation problem do not expect to find such a lucky circumstance in substantively interesting problems. They note typically that wealthy families react differently from poor families to changes in income in terms of consumption behavior. Sociologists usually expect to find such differences, among racial and ethnic groups, for example, in many of the models they employ. Malinvaud [1966] suggests that if the analyst suspects that a single dimension is responsible for major differences between subsets of the sample or population on microparameters, he should do separate analyses for the subgroups defined by this dimension. Within each subset, he would find more nearly constant microparameters if he has correctly identified the dimension disturbing the relationship of interest and if no other important dimension is producing similar results. Sociologists are used to dealing with this very issue in the context of analysis of covariance as interaction effects. We saw in Chapter 4 that Goodman, addressing the problem from a more traditional analysis of covariance considerations, reached the same conclusion as the economists on this matter of variable microparameters.

2. It is also possible for aggregation to be consistent even if all aggregation bias does not disappear. This will be the case when there are exact linear relationships between microvariables and corresponding aggregates:

$$x_{ki}(t) = A_{ki} + B_{ki,k}x_k(t)$$

In other words the coefficients $B_{ki,k'}$ ($k' \neq k$) and the disturbance term in the auxiliary regression are all zero. Examination of equation (5.13) will show that in this case all aggregation bias vanishes from the disturbance term, the constant still depends on noncorresponding parameters β_{ki}, and the macrocoefficients (slopes) are free of dependence on noncorresponding coefficients but are not arithmetic means of the corresponding microcoefficients. The important result is that, since the macroslopes are free of dependence on noncorresponding coefficients (there are no "cross-effects"), aggregation is consistent. This requirement can be interpreted to mean that the micro-explanatory variables must not be linearly related through time with non-corresponding macrovariables. We will consider this issue in some detail below.

3. Finally, it is possible (but unlikely in current sociological research) that there is no exact linear relationship between all of the microvariables and corresponding macrovariables but that we have a theoretical rationale or empirical evidence to suggest that the covariance of $B_{k'i,k}$, β_{ki} is zero in each time period.

These are obviously rather special cases. What of the more general case? Is aggregation bias an inevitable complication? Theil argues that it is not and proposes a strategy of "perfect aggregation." He advocates a peculiar form of *fixed-weight aggregation* which produces macrovariables defined in such a way that aggregation is consistent. Consider the following weighted aggregates (in place of simple sums):

$$y'(t) = \sum_{i=1}^{N} s_i y_i(t) \tag{5.14}$$

$$x'(t) = \sum_{i=1}^{N} w_{ki} x_{ki}(t) \tag{5.15}$$

where s_i and w_{ki} are fixed weights (constants across time periods). We can write the micromodel in the form

$$
\begin{aligned}
s_i y_i(t) &= s_i \alpha_i + \sum_{k=1}^{K} \frac{s_i \beta_{ki}}{w_{ki}} x_{ki}(t) + s_i u_i(t) \\
&= \alpha_i' + \sum_{k=1}^{K} \beta_{ki}'[w_{ki} x_{ki}(t)] + u_i'(t)
\end{aligned}
\tag{5.16}
$$

and see that it is formally equivalent to our earlier unweighted formulation.

To see how fixed-weight aggregation can be consistent by definition, we set the weights s_i equal to unity and assign the following values to w_{ki}:

$$w_{ki} = \frac{\beta_{ki}}{c_{ki}} \quad \text{for all pairs } (k, i)$$

where the c's are arbitrary constants. In other words, we weight micro-variables by the corresponding microparameters. In this case equation (5.16) is reduced to

$$y_i(t) = \alpha_i' + \sum_{k=1}^{K} c_k[w_{ki} x_{ki}(t)] + u_i'(t)$$

so that the microparameters β_{ki}' of equation (5.16) are identically equal to c_k.

This implies that if aggregation is performed such that all microvalues of $x_{ki}(t)$ are weighted proportionately to their microparameters β_{ki}, both the intercept α and the rates of change β_k of the macroequation depend on [corresponding] microparameters only. [Theil 1954, p. 18]

This strategy, while mathematically sound, presents some obvious difficulties from the theory tester's perspective. Lancaster has leveled a compelling criticism at this approach in commenting on the issues in the context of the Keynesian Savings Function:

The definition of Y (the macro-explanatory variable) is not a "natural" definition; it does not conform to any standard statistical series; it is a solution only to the problem at hand and has no special use for any other aggregate income problem; it depends on the exact distribution of income at each period; but it makes the micro- and macro-relationships always consistent. [Lancaster 1966, p. 206]

In other words, the macrocoefficients are dependent on the exact distributions of the microvariables in the population under study for the time period specified. For this reason, the macrocoefficients are sensitive to changes in the distributions of the microvariables across time periods. Similarly, this characteristic of "perfect aggregation" makes it extremely difficult if not impossible to compare macroresults obtained from different populations or in the same population at different time periods.

The theorist presumably operates in terms of general and abstract relationships which are neither time nor place specific. Of course, all operationalizations are to some extent both time and place specific. Yet, this strategy for overcoming time-series aggregation bias seems even more time and population bound than most procedures. In any particular application, "perfect aggregation" is likely to seem highly ad hoc and to have little intuitive or theoretical appeal. None of these criticisms apply, however, to pure prediction applications of the strategy. They are specific to attempts at theory testing or construction.

It appears that consistent aggregation is not easily achieved in practice even in economics. Theil's strategy does not seem, perhaps for the reasons just discussed, to have been widely adopted by economists. Thus, given that we may generally expect at least some aggregation bias in estimates of macroparameters from time series, it is important to examine how this bias is affected by the choice of estimation technique. To this point, we have restricted our attention to ordinary least squares regression analysis. There are, of course, a number of additional linear estimation techniques which sociologists are beginning to explore. Theil's Theorem 7 proves that in the presence of aggregation bias, the macrocoefficients will vary according to the statistical estimation technique.

Suppose that the parameters $\alpha_1\beta_1, \ldots, \beta_k$ of the macroequation (5.3) for the periods $1, \ldots, T$ are estimated from the values $y, x_1, \ldots, x_K$ by a wide class of estimation procedures. Assume further that these estimates are based only on the $K + 1$ values in each time period, i.e., we have no a priori information such as ratios of pairs of slopes, zero covariances, etc. These estimates are represented as follows:

$$\hat{\alpha} = A(y; x_1, \ldots, x_K \mid 1, \ldots, T)$$
$$\hat{\beta}_k = B_k(y; x_1, \ldots, x_K \mid 1, \ldots, T)$$
$$\hat{u}(t) = U(y; x_1, \ldots, x_K \mid 1, \ldots, T)$$

The semicolon between y and x's points to the difference between dependent and explanatory variables, and the time period of observation is denoted by $1, \ldots, T$.

The only restrictions placed on the class of estimation procedures are that "they must be (i) linear in the variable before the semicolon, and (ii) unbiased under the condition that the disturbances of the stochastic equation have zero expectation for any values assumed by the variable behind the semicolon" [Theil 1954, p. 119].

Suppose also that the parameters A_{ki} and $B_{ki,k'}$ of the auxiliary regression (5.8) are estimated by the same procedure so that for all k, i, and k'

$$\hat{A}_{ki} = A(x_{ki}; x_1, \ldots, x_K \mid 1, \ldots, T)$$
$$\hat{\beta}_{ki,k'} = B_{ki}(x_{ki}; x_1, \ldots, x_K \mid 1, \ldots, T)$$

Theil's Theorem 7[6] states that

$$\hat{\alpha} = \sum_{i=1}^{N} \alpha_i + \sum_{i=1}^{N} \sum_{k=1}^{K} \hat{A}_{ki}\beta_{ki}$$
$$= \sum_{i=1}^{N} \alpha_i + \sum_{i=1}^{N} \sum_{k=1}^{K} A(x_{ki}; x_1, \ldots, x_K \mid 1, \ldots, T)$$

$$\hat{\beta}_k = \sum_{i=1}^{N} \sum_{k=1}^{K} \hat{B}_{ki,k'}\beta_{ki} = \sum_{i=1}^{N} \sum_{k=1}^{K} B_{ki}(x_{ki}; x_1, \ldots, x_m \mid 1, \ldots, T)$$

Following Green [1964], we can rewrite the last expression:

$$\hat{\beta}_k = \frac{1}{N} \sum_{i=1}^{N} \beta_{ki} + \sum_{i=1}^{N} \left[B_k(x_{ki}; x_1, \ldots, x_k \mid 1, \ldots, T) - \frac{1}{N} \right] \beta_{ki}$$
$$+ \sum_{i=1}^{N} \sum_{k' \neq k} B_k(x_{ki}; x_1, \ldots, x_K \mid 1, \ldots, T)\beta_{ki}$$

---

[6] See Theil [1954, pp. 119 and 183 ff.] for presentation and proof of this theorem.

and

$$u(t) = \sum_{i=1}^{N} u_i(t) + \sum_{i=1}^{N} \sum_{k=1}^{K} U(x_{ki}; x_1, \ldots, x_K)\beta_{ki}$$

These equations show that the estimated macroparameters are sums of weighted averages (except for the case of the intercept where this is a simple sum) of microparameters. The weights here are the coefficients obtained when the estimation technique in question is applied to the auxiliary regression. Theil concludes:

Hence we can say for the general case of Theorem 7 that the macrointercept is equal to the sum of the microintercepts, and any macroslope is equal to the average of the corresponding (derived) microslopes, both apart from certain covariance corrections. *These covariance corrections are the parts of the macroparameters which are different for different methods of statistical estimation.* [Theil, 1954 p. 122]

This result is not of immediate relevance to sociologists who employ only ordinary least squares procedures. But, as sociologists begin to apply more advanced techniques (such as those discussed in any econometrics text) the implications of this theorem become more cogent. Again, this particular complication is particularly relevant in attempts at comparing studies done on different populations.

This problem is the weakest link in our knowledge of time-series aggregation effects.

The extent to which the failure of the strict conditions for consistent aggregation will lead to unsatisfactory predictions can be discovered only by considering these conditions in relation to the statistical procedure used to estimate the macro-relation. Less has been done on this aspect of the aggregation problem than on the conditions for consistent aggregation themselves. [Green 1964, p. 120]

It is interesting to recast this analysis in causal terms, following Blalock's example. *Examination of* (5.13) *shows that the presence of aggregation bias in the macroparameter estimates depends on nonzero coefficients in the auxiliary regressions relating noncorresponding micro- and macrovariables.* To this point, we have followed the example of the economists who have pioneered in this analysis in considering the auxiliary regressions to be purely formal. But it appears that insight into the aggregation problem arising in time-series estimation can be gained by intensive examination of these relations. The crucial question is, under what conditions are we likely to find microvariables linearly related to noncorresponding macrovariables?[7]

---

[7] We are assuming here that the microparameters are not identical for all microunits. This point will be discussed further when we consider the random-coefficients model.

Theil offers the following explanation:

> . . . the auxiliary equations do not describe their "dependent" variables in an economically significant way. It is certainly true that these variables will usually be positively correlated with the macrovariables corresponding to them—though it is good not to overestimate this correlation—and that they will also be correlated with other macrovariables, because economic variables are usually correlated with each other. [Theil 1954, p. 144]

One possible explanation, then, is that collinearity of the macrovariables is responsible for the appearance of nonzero coefficients joining noncorresponding micro- and macrovariables. But, the coefficients of the auxiliary regression are *partial* regression coefficients. If one or more noncorresponding macrovariables are linearly related to a microvariable only through correlation with the corresponding macrovariable, the partial regression coefficients associated with these macrovariables should be approximately zero. We must look for another explanation. Reference to a simple model is helpful here again. We can revise the model presented in Figure 2-1 to include an arrow connecting one of the microvariables (X_1) with a noncorresponding macrovariable (X'_2), as in Figure 5-1.

If we cannot accept the simple multicollinearity explanation, what shall we propose as an alternative? There seem to be at least three possible explanations for any particular cross-effect: (1) a direct causal relationship from the micro- to the macrovariable through time; (2) a direct causal relationship in the opposite direction; and (3) spurious relationships of noncorresponding micro- and macrovariables due to the operation of one or more variables excluded from the model. Consider the example of the suicide function where we now have a micromodel formulated at the individual level with suicide propensity as the dependent variable and a macromodel formulated at the census-tract level with suicide rate as the dependent variable. It seems highly likely in any extended time series that changes in macro-income will be systematically related to variables such as micro marriage rate and fertility rates (or individual marriage and childbearing decisions). Similarly, if we had included attitudinal variables such as religiosity, radicalism, etc., these also might be systematically related to changes in one of the macrovariables like income or, indeed, marriage rate. In any event, if we estimated the analogous model at the different levels of aggregation, we would obtain inconsistent results due to the cross-effects. The most obvious explanation would be the assumption of direct causal impact from the macrovariables to the microvariables. But there is no basis a priori on which to reject the alternative that changes in microvariables are producing changes in other macrovariables. Addressing this question in any specific case demands

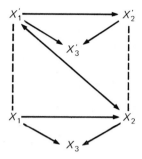

Figure 5-1. Figure 2.1 Revised: Aggregation Bias in a Panel Model.

the formulation of a cross-level theory. We would strongly endorse the statement made by Fox concerning this issue in economics:

> If we are to avoid naive empiricism in dealing with economic aggregates, we must first do some rather careful bridge-building between the *microvariables* and *microrelationships* associated with individual consumers or firms and the *macrovariables* and *macrorelationships* associated with large aggregates of consumers or firms at the national or regional level. [Fox 1968, p. 496]

Quite a few sociologists are willing to make strong arguments for the need of creating theories that include variables from different levels of social structure. There is no point in elaborating on this as the case is strongly made in many of the essays collected by Doggan and Rokkan [1969].

Perhaps the most interesting case is the third listed above. Consider the simple model drawn in Figure 5-2. We see here the possibility that some variable not included in the model, such as level of industrialization, level of political development, or level of any number of cultural variables, may be operating so as to produce a temporal spuriousness between noncorresponding micro- and macrovariables. Thus, the introduction of a time dimension raises the possibility of spuriousness which is not apparent when we restrict our attention to static models estimated at a single point in time.

A Random-Coefficients Model

One of the major recurring themes of the analysis so far has been the extreme importance of population homogeneity for consistency in linear aggregation. In this chapter, we have been very specific in defining such homogeneity (which is often used as a primitive term in verbal discussions of the problems).

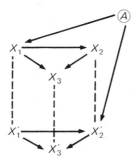

Figure 5-2. An Illustration of "Temporal Spuriousness."

We have seen that consistent aggregation depends on identical slopes for all microunits (i.e., homogeneity in response to changes in explanatory variables in the substantive model under consideration). Both sociologists and economists are understandably troubled by the restrictiveness of this requirement. We will now consider one way of relaxing this assumption so that, under certain conditions, attainment of consistent aggregation is considerably more likely.

Zellner [1969] suggests that we explicitly construct a model incorporating *random* intermicrounit heterogeneity (in a very weak sense).[8] We assume that on the average all micro-units have the same response tendencies with respect to operations of the substantive model but that idiosyncratic differences produce variation around the mean value of such response parameters. In other words, we assume that the coefficients of β_{ki} in equation (5.1) should be represented as follows:

$$\beta_{ki} = \bar{\beta}_k + \delta_{ki}$$

where δ_{ki} is an element from a random distribution with mean zero. Thus, we consider the array of microcoefficients associated with any variable x_k to be N unbiased and independent estimates of the parameter $\bar{\beta}_k$. The micromodel (5.1) can be rewritten to incorporate this modification.

$$y_i(t) = \alpha_i + \sum_{k=1}^{K} (\bar{\beta}_k + \delta_{ki})x_{ki}(t) + u_i(t) \tag{5.17}$$

Theil's procedure at this point would be to define the aggregate variables and *independently* postulate a macrorelation analogous to that of equation

---

[8] It may be unwise to refer to this specification as involving substantive heterogeneity since we specify nothing about interunit differences. Perhaps we should think of the model as one of "weak homogeneity."

(5.17). Zellner follows Klein's [1953] lead in simply summing across the microrelations of (5.17) to obtain a macrorelation which is implied directly by the microrelation. This is an important difference which we have not raised in earlier discussions.[9] We have proceeded on the assumption that, since the sociologist often enough has no control over the aggregation process, Theil's formulation is more useful. This follows from the fact that administrative agencies do not aggregate relations but microobservations. However, as reformulated by Zellner, this approach raises interesting possibilities for sociological applications.

Following Zellner, we then sum the microrelations of (5.17) over all N observations for each time period to obtain

$$\sum_{i=1}^{N} y_i(t) = \sum_{i=1}^{N} \alpha_i + \sum_{i=1}^{N} \sum_{k=1}^{K} \bar{\beta}_k x_{ki}(t) + \sum_{i=1}^{N} \sum_{k=1}^{K} \delta_{ki} x_{ki}(t) + \sum_{i=1}^{N} u_i(t)$$

or

$$y(t) = \alpha + \sum_{k=1}^{K} \bar{\beta}_k x_k(t) + \sum_{i=1}^{N} \sum_{k=1}^{K} \delta_{ki} x_{ki}(t) + u(t) \qquad (5.18)$$

If the δ_{ki} terms are distributed independently of the explanatory variables (and as always the explanatory variables are distributed independently of the disturbance), we can operate on equation (5.18) to produce an unbiased estimate of $\bar{\beta}$, the "underlying" response parameter.[10] In this case, there is as a result no aggregation bias. The estimate of the macrocoefficients are identical with the estimates of the arrays of microcoefficients associated with each variable.

The formulation is still quite restrictive, however. Zellner, like Theil, assumes nonstochastic explanatory variables, i.e., independent variables fixed at some value in the population. For sociological (and most economic) applications we must deal with drawings from joint multivariate distributions of independent and dependent variables, i.e., where both independent and dependent variables are stochastic. But, as Gupta [1969] has pointed out, aggregation analyses haye focused only on the nonstochastic regressor case.

When the explanatory variables are stochastic, the likelihood they will be correlated with the distribution of terms is increased. Since such a correlation introduces aggregation bias, it is essential in any concrete application to assess this possibility. In this sense, Zellner's specification has the same logical status as the requirement in Theil's formulation that the covariance

---

[9] Fox [1968] clearly discusses this strategy and compares it with Theil's approach

[10] Swamy [1970] proves that Aiken's generalized least squares produces consistent and asymptotically efficient estimates of the mean of this distribution as well as unbiased and consistent estimates of the variance–covariance matrix.

terms in (5.13) vanish for consistent aggregation. Zellner points out that the two requirements are not identical. It is difficult to evaluate in the abstract which of the two conditions is more likely to be satisfied in common situations. One would need to examine the detailed implications of each in the context of a substantive model. This does not appear to have been done. The auxiliary theory required to evaluate fit to Zellner's specifications would not be a cross-level model but would concern the partitioning of microunits into classes which behave alike in ways that are influenced by substantive variables in the model.

Summary

No additional aggregation difficulties arise when we estimate a static model at several points in time. We can, however, more clearly specify some of the mechanisms producing aggregation bias since we can more easily think in terms of a microrelation defined uniquely for each microunit. In particular, this enables us to more precisely locate heterogeneity in the population of microunits.

We noted that Theil's strategy of "perfect aggregation," i.e., weighting microvariables by the regression coefficients which relate them to the micro-dependent variables, is useful only for purposes of establishing consistency in empirical prediction problems. The specific nature of such weightings makes the procedure unsuitable for general theory-testing purposes. Examination of the possible kinds of causal structures which could have given rise to such aggregation bias in any particular case gives rise to a different perspective. Attention focuses on cross-level causal processes and on the estimation procedures used. It is particularly important to emphasize the temporal spuriousness possibility just discussed. We have noted in previous chapters the ways in which an aggregation criterion can be differentially related to variables in a model in cross-sectional data. Obviously, the same kind of effect can be produced in using serial observations. The time period defined by the observations may tend to group units in such a way as to produce spurious or partly spurious temporal correlations. And, as in the case of cross-sectional models, omitted variables which produce such effects ("A" in Figure 5-2) may be related to sets of variables in very complicated ways in more complex models. Just as was the case previously, then, we see the need for both cross-level theorizing and detailed knowledge of data.

Finally, the random-coefficients model more adequately represents the analysis situation confronting the analyst than do more conventional regression models. This development is primarily suggestive at the present time as it has not been applied in empirical analysis.

6

Some Complications

To this point we have considered what amount to the simplest problems that arise in aggregation. In particular, we have restricted our attention to single-equation recursive micromodels composed of variables at only one level of analysis. In other words, we implicitly assumed that the micromodel was such that least squares assumptions were satisfied. It is important to consider extensions of the basic results on aggregation to some more complicated situations. Unfortunately, an adequate treatment of such extensions is beyond the scope of this analysis. Since it is important that work in this area be undertaken, we will briefly treat two of the most relevant complicating factors: micromodels which, if fully specified, contain both micro- and macrovariables, and micromodels represented not by a single recursive equation but by a nonrecursive system of equations.

Specification Error

One approach to considering the difficulties which arise when the true micromodel contains variables from both micro- and macrolevels of analysis is to consider the question of errors of specification. In the classical approach to statistical inference, one begins with a sample of observations and assumes or determines that this is a sample of observations from some population.[1] One also assumes some properties of the population and the mechanism which generates samples from it. This set of assumptions is often referred to as the *stochastic specification* or *statistical model*. On the basis of such a specification it is possible to deduce something about the probabilities of obtaining selected values of sample statistics or estimators. Given a knowledge of the sampling distribution (sample-to-sample variability) of the estimators, one may infer something about the unknown interesting features of the population. It is obviously essential for sound inference that the stochastic specification be an appropriate one in the sense that it captures the key features of the process that actually generates the sample data. In statistical inference proper, the model is not questioned. We assume that the stochastic

---

[1] This discussion follows Malinvaud [1966, ch. 2].

specification exactly represents the actual process by which the observed data were generated. The null hypothesis is the only element in the test which is subject to question. If the observed values together with the sampling distribution indicate that this is an extremely improbable sample under the null hypothesis, we reject the null hypothesis, not some other element of the stochastic specification.

The methods of mathematical statistics do not provide us with tools for specifying a statistical model or for choosing between alternative models unless they are embedded in a single more general model (at which point the problem regresses). These are problems of the methodology of the substantive area in which statistics is being employed. For example, consideration of statistical principles will not help us decide whether to use parametric or distribution-free estimators. To make such a decision, one must employ knowledge and insights about the variables under consideration. If theoretical considerations, prior research, and experience suggest that the variables of interest are likely to be approximately normally distributed, we then employ the statistical methods of parametric statistical inference. In other words, the stochastic specification is justified on substantive rather than formal statistical criteria.

The general term *errors of specification* is applied to the differences between the assumptions of the model and the true properties of the data it is assumed to represent. It is obvious that this usage is broad enough to include almost all of the potential pitfalls in statistical inference: sample selection, assumptions about form of relations, neglect of important variables, errors of measurement. It is frequently pointed out that certain of the assumptions of widely used stochastic specifications are not empirically verifiable, e.g., assumptions relating to randomness of errors. The concern for the use and development of robust estimators stems from the recognition that no specification is likely to be perfect and that it is therefore desirable to use estimators whose properties are not highly dependent on the more questionable assumptions of the model.

The term *specification error* has come to be used in a more restricted sense which is directly relevant to problems of aggregation–disaggregation. This kind of error or bias arises when variables that "should" be included in a prediction equation are excluded. There are two important subsets of this type of error: (1) exclusion of variables with important independent causal status, and (2) the inclusion of variables measured with error. We will focus on the first of these since the second topic requires a somewhat complex statistical argument. The interested reader is referred to Theil *et al* [1961] for a treatment of measurement error as specification error.

Before giving substantive examples of specification error compounding aggregation bias, we will briefly develop the effects of specification error of the first type on least squares estimates, since this is not treated in the sociological methodology literature. We follow Goldberger's [1968] concise presentation for the three-variable case.

Consider the regression of y on x_1 and x_2 (assuming that all variables are measured as deviations around their means so as to eliminate the constant term)

$$y = b_{y1.2}x_1 + b_{y2.1}x_2 + e_{y.12} \tag{6.1}$$

Consider further the regression of y on x_1 alone:

$$y = b_{y1}x_1 + e_{y.1} \tag{6.2}$$

The solution for the slope in equation (6.2) may be written in terms of moments.

$$b_{y1} = \frac{m_{1y}}{m_{11}} \tag{6.3}$$

where the m's are moments about the mean:

$$m_{jk} = \sum_{t=1}^{T} (x_{tj} - x_{.j})(x_{tk} - x_{.k}) \qquad j, k = 1, \ldots, K$$

$$m_{jy} = \sum_{t=1}^{T} (x_{tj} - x_{.j})(y_t - y_.) \qquad j = 1, \ldots, K$$

Consider, further, the *auxiliary regression*[2] of x_2 on x_1:

$$x_2 = b_{21}x_1 + e_{2.1} \tag{6.4}$$

where $e_{2.1}$ denotes the residual of the regression of x_2 on x_1. The slope of the auxiliary regression can be written as

$$b_{21} = \frac{m_{12}}{m_{11}} \tag{6.5}$$

In least squares analysis we choose among all possible intercept and slope values by minimizing the error (residual) sums of squares from the regression line (or plane) in a specified direction. When the variables are in deviation form, the two-regressor case involves minimizing

$$S = \sum e^2 = \sum (y - \hat{y})^2 = \sum (y - b_{y1.2}x_1 - b_{y2.1}x_2)^2 \tag{6.6}$$

---

[2] Note that this is a different (but more common) usage of the term from that which we employed in discussing aggregation bias. Here it simply refers to a linear regression among the explanatory variables (regardless of unit of analysis). It is important to note that this auxiliary regression does not imply causal priority of the regressor (x_1) over the regressand (x_2). We simply take the variable omitted from the micromodel as the regressand.

Setting $dS/db_{y1.2} = 0$ gives one of the so-called normal equations:

$$0 = \frac{dS}{db_{y1.2}} = 2\sum (y - b_{y1.2}x_1 - b_{y2.1}x_2)(-x_1)$$

Rearranging and dividing through by 2 gives

$$\sum xy = b_{y1.2}\sum x_1^2 = b_{y2.1}\sum x_1 x_2$$

Since all variables are measured about their means, this is equivalent to

$$m_{1y} = m_{11}b_{y1.2} + m_{12}b_{y2.1} \tag{6.7}$$

into which we can substitute equations (6.3) and (6.5) to obtain

$$b_{y1.2} = b_{y1} - b_{21}b_{y2.1} \tag{6.8}$$

An alternative form of this expression is

$$b_{y1} = b_{y1.2} + b_{21}b_{y2.1} \tag{6.9}$$

This is a useful formulation because, as Goldberger [1968] points out, expression (6.9) gives us an exact answer to the question of what happens if a specific explanatory variable is excluded from a three-variable regression. We could, of course, have carried out a parallel analysis for the exclusion of x_1 from this three-variable regression; in which case, we would have taken x_1 as the regressand in the auxiliary regression.[3] Since we have assumed that the three-variable regression is the correct one, we have implicitly assumed that the population regression function is of the form

$$y = \beta_{y1}x_1 + \beta_{y2}x_2 + \varepsilon$$

We know that if the assumptions necessary for least squares analysis are met, this technique will assure us that $b_{y1.2}$ and $b_{y2.1}$ will be unbiased estimates of the corresponding population parameters β_{y1}, β_{y2}, respectively. Expression (6.9) shows that if the sample data have in fact been generated by a three-variable population regression, b_{y1} (and in the parallel argument, b_{y2}) is a biased estimate of the population parameter β_{y1}. The bias is the magnitude of the difference between b_{y1} and the unbiased estimate $b_{y1.2}$. We can see in (6.9) that this quantity is equal to $b_{21}b_{y2.1}$. We call this bias term, the *specification error* of the coefficient b_{y1}.

Now, to see under what conditions the exclusion of a regressor from a regression analysis will produce specification error in the estimated coefficients in the three-variable regression, we simply consider the conditions under which the specification error $b_{21}b_{y2.1}$ will be nonzero. We see first that

---

[3] The extension of this formulation of specification error to the K-variable case is straightforward using matrix algebra. For such an extension, see Goldberger [1968].

specification error will occur only when the variable excluded "ought" to be included, i.e., when $b_{y2.1} \neq 0$. The excluded variable must have some independent explanatory power (in the statistical sense). In addition, we see that there must be a linear relationship between the variable excluded and the one included, i.e., $b_{21} \neq 0$. Since this specification error term is multiplicative, both conditions must be met for such error to occur. So we see that specification error occurs when the variable excluded has some independent explanatory status of its own and is at the same time linearly related to the variable(s) included.

We note that specification error depends on *multicollinearity* in the sample data. In this sense, specification error can be considered one of the complications arising from multicollinearity. We are referring here to what Johnston [1960] terms *inexact* multicollinearity; the situation in which there is no exact linear relationship among the explanatory variables in a regression (which would make it impossible to identify any of the coefficients), but some subset of the explanatory variables are highly correlated. These high intercorrelations make it difficult to separate out the individual effects of variables, by reducing the efficiency of estimates, in sample data. Multicollinearity is not a problem when the population data are known, and the researcher need not concern himself with this type of specification error unless he suspects that his independent variables are collinear.[4]

There is another way to state this specification problem which may be more intuitively appealing. The crucial assumption for the use of least squares analysis (and, for that matter, any of the techniques deriving from the general linear model) is that the error or disturbance terms of the prediction equation for each observation must be independent of values of the explanatory variables in the prediction equation at that observation. If this assumption is not met, least squares will not, in general, produce unbiased estimates of the parameters of a population regression function. Now, if one excludes a causally important variable from the analysis, the effects of this variable are contained in the disturbance term; i.e., at each observation the effects of this excluded variable on the dependent variable will be considered "error." If, in addition, this excluded variable is highly correlated with one or more of the explicitly considered independent variables, the disturbance term will then necessarily be correlated with these included variables. The resulting bias in the least squares estimates we have termed *specification error*.

Below, we demonstrate that specification error may confound aggregation bias in rather complicated ways. But before moving on to that rather technical

---

[4] For general discussion of this problem stressing relevance to sociological research, see Gordon [1968] and Blalock [1961].

discussion, it is useful to suggest ways in which problems of specification are likely to arise in sociological research. In keeping with general strategy, we will not cite specific examples, but will attempt to show that there is a very general analysis model which suggests a wide class of specification errors in sociological research.[5]

The Structural-Effects Model

The structural or contextual effects model presents an analysis situation that should prove particularly troublesome in aggregation. At the same time, it suggests that, in a wide variety of situations, micromodels which do not contain structural variables are underspecified. This strategy for attempting to assess the effects of group composition or structure on individual behavior and/or attitudes and values seems to have been restricted to the use of means or proportions of microobservations as structural or contextual variables.[6]

The model assumes that variations in the dependent microvariable are produced by changes in both the explanatory microvariables and in one or more analytical contextual variables (i.e., macrovariables). To continue one of Boudon's examples, one might assume that variations through time of individual political behavior are a function of both individual economic position and community economic position (e.g., community per capita income). The implied causal structure is pictured in Figure 6-1. In this figure we use the dot notation to refer to a broad class of linear aggregates rather than to simple sums. As before, we use a dotted line to represent the functional dependence of corresponding micro- and macrovariables.

The model diagrammed in Figure 6-1 can be represented in regression form as follows (if we assume additive linear relations among all variables):

$$y_{it} = \alpha + \beta_{1i}x_{it} + \beta_{2i}x_{\cdot t} + \varepsilon_{it} \tag{6.10}$$

We have already noted that the auxiliary regression joining the two explanatory variables would be expected to have nonzero slope. Since we will be concerned with the exclusion of the structural variable from the micromodel (our previous analyses of aggregation did not allow for variables at more than one level in a given model), the crucial issue is the independent causal

[5] Simon [1968] offers an interesting illustration of the possible specification errors in sociological research likely to arise from neglect of the time-dimension.

[6] Among the most frequently cited uses of the structural-effects model are found in Lipset, Trow, and Coleman [1956]; Blau [1960]; Davis, Spaeth, and Huson [1961]; and Menzel and Katz [1966].

Figure 6-1. Illustration of a Simple Structural-Effects Model.

status of the structural variable. This is a matter of some debate in the discipline.[7]

Let us assume for the sake of argument that some such structural or contextual effect was present in the abstract model we used in demonstrating temporal aggregation bias, i.e., that equation (6.1) was underspecified. The issue becomes: what happens to specification error when an underspecified micromodel is aggregated to a more correctly specified macromodel? We assume here that the macromodel is more correctly specified, although this certainly need not be the case in any realistic example. What this formulation implies then is that community per capita income has an independent causal impact on individual behavior while individual family income has no such effect on community political behavior, and that the aggregation proceeds to the "correct" level, i.e., one employs community-level aggregates.

The reader should suspect by now that the impact of aggregation on specification bias is not likely to be simply analyzed. We are fortunate in this case to be able to draw heavily on a previously published paper. Grunfeld and Griliches [1960] explored a number of aspects of this issue in a seminal paper. We will present their analysis in some detail since we consider their work to have considerable potential relevance to the aggregation problems likely to be addressed by sociologists.

Specification Error and Aggregation Bias

Grunfeld and Griliches argue that economists generally do not know enough about individual economic behavior to perfectly specify microrelations. We

---

[7] For detailed criticism and analysis of this general approach which is sympathetic with the view that structural variables may have independent effects, see Valkonen [1969], Linz [1969] and Scheuch [1969]. For negative criticisms, see Campbell and Alexander [1965] and Hauser [1969].

could, without much objection, extend this charge to the social sciences more generally. The thrust of their paper is the argument that:

Aggregation of economic variables can, and in fact, frequently does, reduce these specification errors. Hence aggregation does not only produce an aggregation error, but it may also produce an aggregation gain. [Grunfeld and Griliches 1960, p. 1]

Grunfeld and Griliches differ from Theil and the other economists already heard from in that they emphasize "power and degree of explanation" rather than estimation of regression (slope) coefficients. This stress on correlation coefficients brings us back closer to current practice in sociological research. Furthermore, they are concerned not with the consistency across levels, but with explaining variation in the macro- or aggregate-dependent variable. In this sense, their analysis is directed at issues quite different from those that motivate the present work. Yet, we will find that their analysis sheds some light on complex issues we are considering as complications. The reader should be aware of the quite distinct differences between the goals that motivated Grunfeld and Griliches and those that motivated Theil. The former have reacted against the stark warnings of the dangers involved in aggregation. Note the title of their paper: "Is Aggregation Necessarily Bad?" They are interested in macroanalysis and see their interests as quite independent of the microtheories or models which might underlie their macro-investigations. The argument basically is that if we cannot assure ourselves of perfectly specified micromodels and our real interest is in macromodel estimation, we should not unduly concern ourselves with aggregation bias. We have taken a different tack in suggesting that, since level of aggregation is a variable, it becomes very important, in comparing research efforts at different levels of aggregation, to consider the likely aggregation bias in coefficients at different levels (given the aggregating techniques employed). This goal is much closer to Theil's than to that of Grunfeld and Griliches. But, as we will see below, Theil assumed perfectly specified micromodels. If we are to make practical use of the results of analyses based on Theil's formulation of the problem, it will be necessary for us to take the results of Grunfeld and Griliches' analysis into account. Thus, although the two kinds of investigations differ greatly in motivation, we can use the results of the latter to modify the findings of the former.

Grunfeld and Griliches employed two previously analyzed sets of data to compare the explanatory power of the aggregate or macrolevel multiple regression with the explanatory power of the microregressions. They found that the aggregate multiple coefficients of determination were in both cases larger in absolute value than any of the microcoefficients. This result of course, is congruent with the results presented in Chapter 3. These authors, suggest, however, that a more relevant measure of the explanatory power of the microregressions (explanatory power relative to the dependent aggregate variable) is obtained by forming a composite of the microregressions. They define a *composite* R^2 as the proportion of the variance in the dependent aggregate variable explained by variation in the composite predicted dependent variable. This latter term denotes the aggregation (according to the rule used in the aggregation process under consideration) of the predicted values of the dependent microvariable from all of the microregressions. We encountered an analogous concept in defining consistency in Chapter 2. There we noted that we could compare the observed dependent macrovariable with the aggregation of predicted microvalues of the dependent variable. We are using "prediction" here in the statistical sense of conditional prediction of the dependent variable given the least squares estimates of the regression coefficients and the sample observations on the independent variables. In each microregression, we could insert each observed value of the independent variable(s) and obtain a predicted value of the dependent variable. Thus for each joint observation of independent variables, we could obtain a predicted value for the dependent variable. The residual or error is defined as the difference between this predicted value and observed value (in the joint observation) of the dependent variable. We obtain the composite dependent variable by aggregating all of these predicted values.

The composite R^2 is calculated in terms of the residuals. We would calculate the residuals from all of the microregressions and aggregate them for each time period and obtain the variance of this aggregate. The reader may wish to think of these aggregates as simple sums, but the logic is applicable to any linear aggregation relation. In any case, we have a measure of unexplained variance in the composite value of the dependent variable. To obtain a measure of explained variance, we divide this quantity by the variance in the dependent aggregate variable and subtract the resulting term from unity. The composite coefficient of determination is expressed symbolically as

$$R_c^2 = 1 - \frac{S_c^2}{S_y^2}$$

where S_c^2 denotes the variance of the composite dependent variable and S_y^2, the variance of the observed aggregate dependent (which, remember, is an analytical variable, i.e., it is some linear transformation of the dependent microvariables).

The *aggregate* R^2 is defined in the usual manner, i.e., we simply replace

S_c^2 in the above expression with S_a^2, the variance in the dependent aggregate variable explained by the aggregate or macroregression

$$R_a^2 = 1 - \frac{S_a^2}{S_y^2}$$

Given these two expressions, we can express the relation between the aggregate and composite coefficients of determination as

$$R_c^2 = 1 - \frac{S_c^2}{S_a^2}(1 - R_a^2) \qquad (6.11)$$

which is derived as follows:

$$R_c^2 = 1 - \frac{S_a^2}{S_y^2}$$

$$= 1 - \frac{S_c^2}{S_y^2}\frac{S_a^2}{S_a^2}$$

$$= 1 - \frac{S_c^2}{S_a^2} + \frac{S_c^2}{S_a^2} - \frac{S_c^2}{S_y^2}\frac{S_a^2}{S_a^2}$$

$$= 1 - \frac{S_c^2}{S_a^2} + \frac{S_c^2}{S_a^2}\left(1 - \frac{S_a^2}{S_y^2}\right)$$

$$= 1 - \frac{S_c^2}{S_a^2} + \frac{S_c^2}{S_a^2}R_a^2$$

$$= 1 - \frac{S_c^2}{S_a^2}(1 - R_a^2)$$

Equation (6.11) shows that the relation between the two measures depends on the relation between the variance of the composite residual and the aggregate residual. In their empirical studies, Grunfeld and Griliches obtained aggregate R^2's which were larger than the composite R^2's. Thus they conclude that they did not lose explanatory power as a result of aggregation bias in using the aggregate regression. That is, if they were interested in predicting the dependent aggregate variable, they would have gained nothing by disaggregation.

In the technical part of their paper, Grunfeld and Griliches address the two issues already raised: (1) what factors account for the magnitude of R_a^2 relative to R_i^2, the microcoefficient of determination; and (2) what factors determine the size of R_a^2 relative to R_i^2.

Their answer to the first question is essentially the same as that proposed by the sociologists and considered in Chapter 3. Since their different emphasis results in a useful formalization of the issue, we will briefly consider their analysis. Grunfeld and Griliches cite the operation of a *synchronization effect* (what we called the clustering effect). This is defined as follows:

The higher the correlation between the independent variables of different individuals or behavior units, certibus paribus, the higher the R^2 of the aggregate equation relative to the R^2's of the microequations. [Grunfeld and Griliches 1960, p. 4]

To show how the increase in correlation coefficients with grouping depends on clustering or synchronization, they employ the following restricted model. Consider the microequation $y_{it} = bx_{it} + u_{it}$ where all variables are measured as deviation about their means. Assume that all individuals can be represented by a model with a constant coefficient (in which case aggregation will be consistent); and further assume that the variance of x_{it}, s_{xi}^2, is constant for all observations and that the variance of u_{it}, s_{ui}^2, is constant for all i. The inflation effect we are concerned with depends on the intercorrelations of observations on the independent variables and on the intercorrelations of the disturbances. In this simple model, Grunfeld and Griliches assume that the intercorrelations among microunits on the independent variable and on the disturbance term, ρ_x and ρ_u respectively, are the same for all parts of individuals. Both correlation coefficients denote the correlation of observed values for pairs of microunits from a time series, i.e., for microunits i and j we have T observations on variables $x_{it}(t = 1, \ldots, T)$. The assumption that the value of such "synchronization coefficients" is the same for all pairs of microunits is equivalent to the assumption that the causal influences and random shocks which are operating across time but not included in the model have the same impact on all pairs of microunits. It helps in following this argument to visualize a number of such effects operating across time and producing systematic variations in micro-X and Y values. Under these restrictive assumptions, the ratio of R_a^2 to R_i^2 can be expressed as[8]

$$\frac{R_a^2}{R_i^2} = \frac{b^2 S_{xi}^2 + S_{ui}^2}{b^2 S_{xi}^2 + S_{ui}^2 \dfrac{1 + (N - 1)\rho_u}{1 + (N - 1)\rho_x}} \tag{6.12}$$

This expression makes clear that the relationship of interest (macro- vs. microcoefficient of determination) depends in this restrictive case on the relative size of ρ_x and ρ_u.

Grunfeld and Griliches also demonstrate that this analysis can be extended

---

[8] A rather extended derivation of this result is presented in Grunfeld and Griliches [1960, Appendix A].

to the cross-sectional case in which the appropriate "coefficient of synchronization" is the intraclass correlation coefficient. In this case, expression (6.12) is modified by simply replacing the time series coefficients ρ_x and ρ_u with the intraclass correlation coefficients r_x and r_u.

The unique contribution of Grunfeld and Griliches to the analysis of this issue is to point out that the relative size of the micro- and macrocoefficients of determination depends on the specification of the micromodel. In a perfectly specified model, the disturbance term would be composed of truly "random shocks." That is, if all of the causally important variables have been included in the micromodel, we would expect that the disturbance term would be composed of the offsetting effects of numerous weak causal influences. If this were the case, it would be highly unlikely that any aggregating criterion variable would systematically affect the disturbance term thus producing a large ρ_u term. That is, we would expect that ρ_u would be approximately zero for all pairs of observations. Thus, in the perfectly specified case, all that is needed for R_a^2 to be greater than R_i^2 is a positive synchronization (intercorrelation) of microunits on the explanatory variable (i.e., $\rho_x > 0$).

In most practical applications, we would not expect perfect specification. Thus, in the general case, we must concern ourselves with the size of ρ_x relative to ρ_u. The size of the latter depends on the incompleteness of the model. The more the disturbance term is dominated by one important causal variable excluded from the model, the more likely it is that ρ_u will be large relative to ρ_x. This of course will happen only when the excluded variable is systematically related to the aggregation-criterion variable. It is also possible to obtain large ρ_u values relative to ρ_x when the disturbance term is composed mainly of several excluded variables all or most of which are systematically related in similar ways to the aggregation criterion. The probability of obtaining ρ_u large relative to ρ_x decreases as it becomes more likely that the disturbance term is composed of a large number of excluded variables. This is reasonable since the more effects contained in the disturbance term, the less likely it is that all of them will be systematically related to the aggregation criterion in similar ways (e.g., positively vs. negatively related). Expression (6.12) shows that all that is required for the inflation of the R_a^2 relative to R_i^2 is that ρ_x be greater in value than ρ_u. In any particular case, addressing this question will involve a detailed examination of the possible specification imperfections in the micromodel according to the principles just illustrated. The reader who wishes to consider this argument in greater detail is referred to the various appendixes of the Grunfeld and Griliches. They demonstrate that this result, dependent on very restrictive assumptions, is not contradicted as the assumptions are relaxed, e.g., as we allow unequal variances, variable regression coefficients, multivariate relations, etc.

We have already noted that it is more meaningful to compare R_a^2 with the composite coefficient of determination. We cannot use the synchronization argument to explain the observed difference between R_a^2 and R_c^2 since synchronization affects both measures in the same way.

It is a curious fact that one aggregate regression can offer a better explanation of the variability of the aggregate dependent variable than the combined results of a large number of micro-regressions. At first glance, it looks as if the micro-equations contain all the information contained in the macro-equation and more—how then can the macro-equation give a "better" explanation? [Grunfeld and Griliches 1960, p. 6]

We should again note that Grunfeld and Griliches are using explanation in the restricted statistical sense of conditional prediction or "variance accounted for." Now, since R_a^2 and R_c^2 have the same denominator, S_y^2, *we are interested in conditions under which the variance of the residuals of the macroequation will be smaller than the variance of the aggregate* (sum, in this analysis) *of the residuals of the microregressions.*

To investigate this question, Grunfeld and Griliches employed Theil's formulation. In particular, they take the variance of the expression for the macroresidual in terms of microresiduals and noncorresponding terms.[9]

$$u(t) = \sum_{i=1}^{N} u_i(t) + \sum_{i=1}^{N} \sum_{k=1}^{K} \beta_{ki} V_{ki}(t) \qquad (6.13)$$

The variance of this macroresidual is as follows:

$$E[u(t)^2] = \text{var}\left[\sum_{i=1}^{N} u_i(t) + \sum_{i=1}^{N} \sum_{k=1}^{K} \beta_{ki} V_{ki}(t) \right] \qquad (6.14)$$

where $u(t)$ is the calculated disturbance in the macroregression at time t; $u_i(t)$ is the disturbance in the ith microregression at time t; β_{ki} is the coefficient of the microregression (associated with the kth variable in the ith regression); and $V_{ki}(t)$ is the disturbance of the auxiliary regression of $x_{ki}(t)$ on all of the explanatory macrovariables. This last term is of central importance. Theil had noted earlier that:

This expression is always larger than the variance of the sum of the micro-disturbances, unless the non-stochastic part of the right hand side of [our (6.13)] vanishes. . . . *In general the second moment about zero of a macro-disturbance is larger than the variance of the sum of the corresponding micro-disturbances.* [Theil 1954, p. 115]

---

[9] This equation is derived in Chapter 5, expression (5.9).

Obviously, this conclusion is contradicted by the empirical studies carried out by Grunfeld and Griliches. They proceed to point out that this contradiction is only apparent since Theil's conclusions are correct within the framework of his assumptions. The relevant assumptions are (1) that the explanatory microvariables are nonstochastic i.e., they are predetermined and fixed; and (2) that the microequations are perfectly specified. If these assumptions are met, equation (6.14) reduces to

$$E[u(t)^2] = \text{var}\left[\sum_{i=1}^{N} u_i(t)\right] + \left[\sum_{i=1}^{N} \sum_{k=1}^{K} \beta_{ki} V_{ki}(t)\right] \qquad (6.15)$$

and since the right-most term in this expression is nonnegative, it is clear that $E[u(t)^2]$, the variance of the macroresidual, must be greater than or equal to the variance of the sum of the microresiduals. The two quantities are equal only when there is no aggregation bias. However, this simplification depends on the first assumption listed above. If the assumptions are not met, the analysis is somewhat more complicated. It is more interesting for our purposes to focus on the second assumption.

We have already established that if the microequations are not perfectly specified, the microresiduals will contain an additional term, the specification bias. Thus, the obtained microresiduals will be larger than the "true" microresiduals. The macroresidual is inflated over the sum of the "true" microresiduals, and the obtained microresiduals are inflated over the "true" microresiduals. Thus, *the relationship of the variance of the residuals from the aggregate equation to the variance of the sum of the obtained microresiduals (from the underspecified microequations) will depend on the size of the aggregation bias relative to the specification bias.*

In the course of a further formalization and technical argument (which we will not reproduce here as it would unduly lengthen and complicate this presentation), Grunfeld and Griliches consider the conditions under which the specification error is likely to be greater than the aggregation error. They demonstrate that (at least for relatively simple models) the crucial factor is the relative importance of the excluded macrovariable in the microequation. As we would expect, the greater the causal importance of the excluded macrovariable relative to the included explanatory microvariables in the micromodel, the more likely it is that specification error will be greater than aggregation error, and R_a^2 will tend to be larger than R_c^2. But, we know from the results presented in Chapters 3 and 5 that aggregation bias is partly a function of the number of microrelations over which aggregation is performed (considering that each observation on the dependent microvariable is associated with an individual micromodel). Thus the greater the number of microrelations over which aggregation is performed, the more important do the excluded macrovariables have to be relative to the included microvariables for specification error to be greater than aggregation error. One result which is not immediately apparant, given previous results, and which in fact, contradicts the finding relative to the comparison of R_a^2 and R_i^2, is that the greater the intercorrelation of values on the independent variables (synchronization) the less the expected difference between R_a^2 and R_c^2. It is important to point out that if all of the individuals can be assigned the same micromodel (i.e., the microcoefficients are constants), the aggregation bias will vanish but the specification error will not. As a corollary, the wider the dispersion of the microcoefficients is, the larger will be the aggregation bias relative to the specification bias.

Given their concern for prediction of the aggregate- or macro-dependent variable as opposed to concern for consistency of predictions on more than one level of aggregation, Grunfeld and Griliches respond firmly in the negative to the question posed in the title of their paper: aggregation is not *necessarily* bad. It is even possible to experience an *aggregation gain* in estimating simply the aggregate regression rather than considering the microregressions. Of course, such an aggregation gain occurs only when the specification error (exclusion of an explanatory *aggregate* variable) is greater than the aggregation error. Our concern, of course, is somewhat different. We are more concerned with comparing results obtained on different levels of aggregation than with evaluating the ability of models at different levels to explain variance in the dependent macrovariable. What, then, is the relevance of the Grunfeld-Griliches analysis to our larger aims?

This analysis is most useful in pointing up one of the fundamental limitations of the consistency framework. We have seen to this point that there are a number of issues involved in aggregation which may be efficiently addressed by employing the restrictive assumptions embodied in the consistency requirement. Yet it is important to note the limited applicability of this framework. Consider the illustration we employed in discussing the structural-effects model. We took a micromodel that had changes in individual income and in some aggregate income variable, say per capita income, producing changes in individual political radicalism through time. Now the reason for discussing such a model is the implication that it is often the case that the macrovariable will be omitted from the micromodel. In our usual analysis of aggregation effects, we would compare the micromodel which excludes the macrovariable with a macromodel in which, for example, average political radicalism score through time in some collectivity is taken as a function of changes in average income. The results presented in this section demonstrated that this aggregation would compound aggregation bias with specification error. Furthermore, we cannot obtain independent estimates of the specification bias and the aggregation bias. But what does aggregation bias mean in this context? The formulation implies that the macromodel is not underspecified. Thus, in order to consider aggregation bias we must study the consistency between an underspecified micromodel and a better specified macromodel. Unless one were blindly following some proposed analytical procedure, he would not be interested in establishing such consistency. By the same token, if the analyst had begun with an improved micromodel containing the macrovariable, he would no longer have a one-to-one correspondence of micro- to macrovariables. This is not to imply that we would never be interested in considering the possible consistency of "noncorresponding" micro- and macromodels. Such a question simply cannot be addressed within the framework of the consistency approach as it has been defined here. This kind of issue will eventually have to be handled if many substantively interesting aggregation problems are to be adequately resolved. Such analyses would involve both the extension and modification of the approaches arising from concerns with consistency as well as approaches which are as of yet untried. We should emphasize that many of these kinds of problems are not purely empirical or methodological. There is a conspicuous lack of theoretical models available to provide guidelines in such analyses. Substantial theoretical as well as methodological advance will be required for the satisfactory resolution of many of the issues we have raised.

That we should try to eliminate specification error is obvious. But what of the aggregation problems arising in research as it is currently practiced? Is the Grunfeld-Griliches analysis relevant here? We think so. Firstly, it is important for sociologists to be aware of the potentially complicating effects of specification error. For the kind of specification error we have considered to be operative, it is necessary that one or more explanatory variables from the more macro level have an independent causal impact in the more micro equation and that the excluded variable(s) be correlated with one or more of those included. The crucial issue here is the question of the independent causal status of macrovariables in micromodels. As we noted above, there is a great deal of controversy over this question among sociologists at the current time.

Aggregation in Nonrecursive Models

To this point, we have confined the analysis to single-equation models at more than one level of aggregation. Since sociologists are seldom content with such limited models, it is important to consider application of the analysis of the preceding chapters to such models. Unfortunately we will not be able to do anything more than to illustrate the problems involved. No one has, as yet, adequately handled the aggregation problems involved in multiequation models except for the special case of recursive systems of simultaneous equations.[10] In such models, each equation represents a single endogenous variable as a function of a set of exogenous (from the perspective of the equation in question) variables. It is easy to imagine the construction of macroequations corresponding to each of the equations in the micro-recursive system exactly as such aggregation was described for single-equation models in Chapter 2. Indeed, recursive models are peculiar specifically in that individual equations in the model may be treated discretely in a statistical analysis. There are thus no peculiar difficulties in assessing the consistency between equations in a microrecursive model and corresponding equations in a macrorecursive model. All of the results of previous chapters are also applicable to this case.

The peculiar problems arise when we allow for two-way causation and complex interdependencies in our micromodels. Given that sociologists tend strongly to employ such complexities on the theoretical level, it seems likely that sociologists will follow the lead of economists and employ nonrecursive systems of simultaneous equations to represent their models. This will mean that we will have to move beyond ordinary least squares to more complicated estimation techniques. All of our analyses will become more complex. Since we have seen that every complication (variable regression coefficients, N-variable models, specification error) introduced greatly complicated the analysis of aggregation bias, the reader should suspect that the shift from one-equation models to systems of simultaneous equations will greatly increase the seriousness of the aggregation problem.

An adequate discussion of the issues involved would require a considerable amount of development. We will limit ourselves here to a brief statement of the additional complexities involved and reference to the relevant literature. The analysis situation is one in which we have a model specified as a system of simultaneous equations for all of the individual units in the study population or sample. We want to compare the estimates obtained from estimating this model with the estimates obtained from an analogous system in macro-variables. Theil [1954, 1959] has formulated the following strategy. The system of microequations, which we will call the system of *microstructural*

---

[10] The peculiarity of recursive models, from the standpoint of aggregation analysis, involves the introduction of lagged endogenous variables. Lagged endogenous variables may complicate the meaning of "corresponding" in the expression "corresponding parameters." A consideration of one or more such models will show that we have to extend the notion of correspondence to explicitly include the lags built into the model. For examples, see Theil [1954, ch. 4].

equations contains both predetermined and jointly determined variables. The first step is to reduce this to a system in which the jointly determined variables depend only on predetermined variables. The resulting system is called the *microreduced form*. At this point we can apply aggregation procedures to all of the variables in the microreduced form to obtain the *macroreduced form*. This clearly is equivalent to the procedure employed in the single-equation situation since each "dependent" variable depends only on predetermined variables. To this point, we have introduced no new aggregation problems. The difficulty arises in the attempt to move from the macroreduced form to the system of *macrostructural equations*. Theil has demonstrated that (as one would expect) the feasibility of making this transformation depends on the identifiability of the micro- and macro-models. If the models are not identified, there are an infinite number of ways in which this transformation can be made. If the models are just identified, the transformation can be made in principle although the procedures introduce new complexities. Finally, if the models are over identified, the transformation is extremely difficult in practice. Theil has suggested an approach to the reduction or elimination of aggregation bias in the estimation of the macrostructural equations. This, however, demands that a number of highly restrictive assumptions be met. Further, even this complicated procedure produces only asymptotic reductions in the aggregation bias so that we would have no confidence in estimates drawn from small or moderately large samples. There has been very little further analysis of the additional aggregation difficulties introduced by the shift to systems of simultaneous equations, perhaps because the issues raised in aggregation in single-equation models are still so far from being resolved. The reader is referred to Fisher [1962] for another view of the problem of aggregation in this situation.

Standardized vs. Unstandardized Coefficients

There is something of a split currently in sociology between those who employ standardized regression techniques (principally path analysis) and those who advocate the use of unstandardized regression techniques.[11] The analyses of econometricians have been focused on the estimation of unstandardized regression coefficients and to a lesser degree on correlation coefficients which, of course, are standardized. As yet, there are no analyses of the effects of aggregation on standardized regression coefficients. We should note that it is technically incorrect to apply path analysis to averages or other

---

[11] For a comparison of the two strategies which favors unstandardized strategies, see Blalock [1968].

transformations of the directly measured units.[12] Yet, social scientists often find themselves in the position of working with data which do not meet all of the assumptions for certain statistical procedures. As indicated above, this situation makes studies of robustness particularly important from our perspective. As far as we can determine there have been no studies of the effects of violating this assumption. We know that path coefficients represent a measure which shares some of the properties of both unstandardized regression coefficients and correlation coefficients. Path coefficients, like other standardized measures, depend on the population variability of the variables in the model. We have seen that aggregation tends to affect the variation in variables differentially (depending on the causal relations between the aggregating criterion and the other variables in the model). If this is the case in any particular application, we would expect the obtained coefficients to vary widely at different levels under different kinds of aggregating procedures. At the present time, we do know how serious this aggregation bias is likely to be in substantively interesting analysis situations. This would be an interesting subject for a simulation study. Such a simulation would involve constructing simple models with various levels of known aggregation bias (creating by varying variation in micro- and macrovariables so as to vary the strength of relations in the auxiliary regressions) and comparing the estimates of path models with unstandardized procedures. Of course, the difficulty here, as usually is the case with simulations, is deciding on an empirically realistic range of aggregation bias.

---

[12] For a brief discussion of this point, see Wright [1968].

7 Conclusions

We have summarized most of the technical discussions as we have proceeded. We realize, however, that it may be difficult to draw practical conclusions in the face of such a mass of detail. So we briefly restate here the major results which have import for the conduct of empirical research and then go on to suggest extensions of the methodological analysis.

The consistency formulation with its explicit focus on the logical interrelations of micro-, macro- and aggregation relations provides a convenient vehicle for organizing a variety of aggregation–disaggregation complications. It has the virtue of providing a clear measure of what we have called aggregation bias. We argued in this context that the substantive interpretation one gives to such bias depends largely on one's substantive concerns and metatheoretical outlook. Despite this, the consistency model provides a straightforward means of determining the extent to which aggregation rules affect parameter estimates of analogous functional specifications at different levels of aggregation.

The consistency criterion has direct practical utility when the analyst has control over the aggregation relations (i.e., can determine the grouping criteria). In such cases, it provides a means of assessing "loss of information" with aggregation. More concretely, Nataf's theorem constrains the analyst to attempt aggregation in the interest of economy of representation only when all the relationships involved are linear or to transform nonlinear relations to a linear form if possible. In addition, the functional separability formulation (Leontief) constrains the grouping of variables (as distinct from the grouping of observations on variables).

We have been more concerned with the complications that arise when a sociologist has no control over the grouping procedures and faces the task of using data organized at a level of aggregation inappropriate to his substantive concerns. An analogous difficulty appears when we focus on the "ecology" of research activity. Sociologists are often faced with the problem of comparing research results on similar formulations analyzed at different levels of aggregation. The practical problem in these cases is making a judgment on the degree to which aggregation has distorted functional relations holding on the microlevel. In some cases, this arises in the form of a disaggregation problem: how safe is it in a particular case to infer some microrelation from an observed macrorelation? In other cases, as an aggregation problem: given that we observe different results at various levels of aggregation, should we attribute the differences to aggregation complications or to substantive problems in the postulation of the same model to different levels?

By far the most important insight into the effects of aggregation is the realization that such shifts are likely to systematically change the variation in the substantive variables under consideration. Depending on the specific situation, this can confound variation in explanatory variables, or in explanatory and residual (latent) variables, or produce "spurious" relationships among substantive independent and dependent variables. It is, therefore, extremely important to understand the conditions under which each of the effects are most likely. It will be simplest to summarize the effects on correlation coefficients and regression coefficients separately.

The effects of grouping or aggregation on correlation coefficients are easily summarized. Only under the (usually) unrealistic assumption that values of the variables are distributed randomly or uniformly on the dimension (spatial, temporal, organizational, etc.) on which the aggregation is performed, or that the population is homogeneous, will correlation coefficients remain relatively invariant with grouping. We have seen that in most interesting cases, the inflation of such coefficients is likely to be extreme. The degree of inflation depends on the degree of clustering or synchronization. It is obvious that inferences from aggregate or ecological correlations to what we have called microcorrelations, are made with great risk of error. In Chapter 4, we considered several techniques which partially resolve this particular disaggregation problem. A general conclusion from this is that one needs to make substantive assumptions in order to intelligently approach such disaggregation problems. Finally, almost all discussions of the effects of grouping on correlation coefficients are restricted to the bivariate case. We have considerable difficulty making general statements about the effects of grouping on multiple and partial correlation coefficients. However, the discussion of Chapters 3 and 6 is helpful in suggesting guidelines. In any event, one should always be wary of making cross-level inferences from correlation coefficients.

More troubling from the perspective of advance in quantitative model construction and testing are the well-documented effects of levels changes on regression coefficients. Since correlation coefficients behave symmetrically with respect to changes in the variability of either independent or dependent variables, we do not have to be specific about which variables are most affected by the aggregation process. However, this concern is crucial in attempting to unravel the effects of aggregation on regression (slope) estimates.

We can see again in this case that the homogeneity of the population of microunits (defined specifically in terms of the behavioral relations represented in the model under consideration) enters in an important way. If microvalues are distributed randomly on the dimension on which grouping is performed, then variation in all variables should be affected in the same way and regression coefficients will not be biased (although their statistical efficiency is reduced). We considered homogeneity from two different perspectives. In cross-sections, we considered clustering of values either areally or organizationally. In the time series or panel case, where behavioral reactions of each microunit can be estimated, we defined homogeneity in terms of identical reactions to changes in substantive variables for all microunits. Although the second usage is clearer, the implications of each case are identical.

The issue of microhomogeneity is particularly problematic when the microobservations are missing (i.e., in disaggregation). The issue of homogeneity is defined not only in terms of a substantive model but also concretely in terms of variation in the particular population under study. Thus, additional information must be introduced into the analysis to inform the researcher as to the likelihood that the population he is studying is homogeneous for his purposes. Very often this subsidiary information must be taken from studies on different micropopulations. This follows from the assumption that a researcher would not be likely to be involved in complicated aggregation–disaggregation problems if he had this much detailed information on his micropopulation.

The most interesting and most serious aggregation–disaggregation problems arise in the case of microheterogeneity. In this case, the grouping procedure applied by some third party (usually an administrative unit) will usually have differential effects on substantive variables in the model. Blalock demonstrated for the bivariate case that grouping which does not directly affect the dependent variable will not bias regression estimates, but that grouping which does affect the dependent variable directly will produce specification error in the macrorelation and will thus bias the regression estimates. Alker has extended this thinking to suggest that grouping may systematically produce covariation at the macrolevel between a dependent variable and an independent variable which are neither causally related nor correlated at the microlevel.

The focus on bivariate relations limits the types of aggregation complications which can arise. When we consider multivariate models, we see that slope estimates can in fact be biased by grouping procedures which operate directly on independent variables by confounding variation in these variables. In the bivariate case, variation in the one independent variable could become

114

confounded only with either the disturbance term (representing a set of variables excluded from the model) or the dependent variable. In more complex cases, the regression estimate attached to any single independent variable can become inflated or deflated as variation in that variable is confounded with variation in other independent variables. Theil's representation of aggregation bias in a time series analysis of a static model provides a case in point. The aggregation bias in this case is composed of linear combinations of coefficients of noncorresponding independent variables. In other words, the bias results from a confounding of the effects of independent variables. As the discussion of this particular case demonstrates, the task of unraveling aggregation complections in a multivariate model may be quite formidable.

While the consistency formulation is very useful for the purposes listed above, a careful examination of the implications of Grunfeld-Griliches' analysis points to some significant limitations. The bulk of methodological work in this area has assumed both nonstochastic explanatory variables and perfect specification of the microrelations.[1] Sociologists do not need to be reminded of the stringency of these assumptions for their research. The relaxation of the perfect-specification assumption raises some interesting possibilities for cross-level models. The limitation of the consistency formulation here is that it does not lend itself to the analysis of models in which variables from more than one level of aggregation appear in any substantive relation. Much additional work in this area is needed.

We have argued that the successful resolution of aggregation–disaggregation problems depends on two kinds of developments. The first is the formulation of fairly abstract representations of the ways in which specific grouping criteria or aggregation relations affect microprocesses. At present, we tend to rely wholly on empirical generalizations about the clustering of values of variables areally and temporally. The extensions we call for should employ knowledge of social structure and process to specify the ways in which grouping will affect variation in variables in selected social (micro) processes. The second kind of development involves cumulation of the specific information needed to apply these abstract models to specific instances. Here the concern would be with levels of variation in variables, "strength" of associations,[2] composition of the residual or disturbance term, etc. We suggested above that this type of activity must depend at least in part on the results of

---

[1] We have not treated the issue of stochastic explanatory variables systematically. The sociological analyses we follow do not in general assume nonstochastic explanatory variables. Gupta [1969] shows the great difficulty involved in relaxing the nonstochastic-variable restriction and the perfect-specification restriction simultaneously.

[2] Cf. Shively [1969].

microanalysis conducted on different populations of units (again we emphasize that we do not restrict microunits to being actors, they may be organizations, regions, etc.). Both types of work proceed on the premise that work at different levels of aggregation must not be disjoint but that effective resolution of problems encountered in shifting levels depends largely on the existence of satisfactory theoretical and measurement models and careful empirical work at a number of levels. We noted in the first chapter that levels of aggregation are not isomophic with levels of analysis. Yet, it seems likely that conceptual and theoretical work at more than one analytic level is needed in the satisfactory resolution of general levels of aggregation problems.

At a number of points in the previous chapters we have noted areas where the present state of knowledge on aggregation–disaggregation complications is particularly weak and have suggested additional investigations. Here we will do little more than list the most interesting of these.

1. Little is known of the magnitude of aggregation bias in all but a very limited number of cases. Almost all previous empirical work in sociology (e.g., Robinson, Blalock, Shively, Slatin) has focused on bivariate relations. Boot and deWit [1960] present the only multivariate analysis in economics we have seen. It is obviously very important for us to be able to roughly calculate the magnitude of aggregation bias for a variety of interesting cases. The work to be done here would ideally involve both empirical analysis and Monte Carlo type simulation.

2. Even less is known of the formal consequences of aggregation in nonrecursive models. Given the difficulties we have in specifying the precise nature of aggregation complications for recursive models when the grouping relations are unconstrained, this is not surprising. Yet, there are substantive trends in our discipline which make the study of the nonrecursive case quite important. Many of the most interesting aggregation problems involving the reconciliation of empirical findings from different levels of aggregation arise in what is loosely called macrocomparative research. One of the characteristics of most of our macromodels is our inability to specify asymmetric causal relations. There is more reliance here than in most areas of the discipline on ideas of "mutual causation." This suggests that recursive models may not often be appropriate in research guided by present theorizing in this area. And, while we feel that macro theorists must continue to attempt to further specify precise relationships among the variables which interest them; for the present, the aggregation difficulties that do arise are likely to arise in the context of quite complex nonrecursive models.

3. The spectral analysis approach to aggregation–disaggregation problems briefly outlined in Chapter 3 is extremely intriguing. This method ought to be applied to sets of areal and temporally located microdata aggregated in

different ways and at different levels of consolidation to compare the precision with which spectral analysis locates the source of aggregation complications with that achieved here with more conventional linear models techniques.

4.   This raises another interesting direction of movement. We commented several times on the concentration of interest of aggregation theorists on areal and temporal aggregation. A generally useful theory of aggregation demands an understanding of grouping on social structural dimensions other than spatial–temporal location. Obviously much of such development awaits more satisfactory abstract representations of social structure. However, it seems unwise to delay the beginnings of this work until such a representation is achieved. Indeed, there is reason to believe that the achievement of an understanding of the issue posed would constitute a considerable advance in understanding the formal properties of social structure. One of the interesting possibilities involves locating microunits in N-dimensional "social structural" space (where N is hopefully some small number) and applying spectral analysis and a formal consistency analysis to the grouping problems (outlined in earlier chapters) defined in this context.

5.   In the second chapter we took pains to analytically separate aggregation complications from measurement concerns. At some point, however, we must study the intersection of the two problems. This is a particularly pressing concern in the case of measurement models for macrostructural variables.[3]

---

[3] See the discussions by Hannan [1970b], and Blalock [1971].

Appendix A

Review of Some Elementary Calculus

The aggregation analyses appearing in the literatures of other disciplines, particularly economics, demand of the reader a rather thoroughgoing familiarity with the calculus. Any appreciation of the systematic nature of the economic analyses of the aggregation problem requires an understanding of the mathematical formulation of the problem. A heuristic development of the mathematical statement is presented in Chapter 2.

The key results stated in Chapter 2 require at the very minimum, an elementary knowledge of the calculus of derivatives and differentials. The purpose of this appendix is to present in summary form the mathematical results necessary for the appendix which follows. We would like to make it clear that this summary is intended as nothing more than an aid to understanding the second chapter. In particular, we have not adopted the rigorous approach necessary for precise mathematical exposition, nor have we incorporated the detail desirable for a full understanding of the concepts employed. The reader is strongly urged to consult one or more of the sources cited below for a more detailed and precise treatment.

There are any number of introductory calculus texts available. These may prove somewhat frustrating to the interested social scientist since they stress elegance of statement rather than relevance of results and since the applications presented are usually exclusively drawn from the physical sciences. Fortunately, there are now a number of works available in the field of mathematical economics which cover the same ground (or at least that part of it which is relevant to economic theorizing) at a level which is more appropriate for the social scientist. This appendix draws heavily from these works. We would particularly recommend Archibald and Lipsey [1967], *An Introduction to a Mathematical Treatment of Economics.* I have closely followed their development in this appendix. The reader is also referred to Kooros [1965] and to the classic in this field by Allen [1938]. Finally, at a more advanced level, the reader is referred to Hoffman [1970], particularly Chapter 7.

The reader with statistical training is familiar with linear functions of the form

$$y = a + bx \tag{A.1}$$

where a is called the intercept and b the slope. Slope is a geometric concept and represents the direction and magnitude of changes in y (called the dependent variable) associated with changes in x (the independent variable).[1] More generally, the slope of a curve at any point on the curve is the slope of a straight line tangent to the curve at that point. A linear function is graphed as in Figure A-1.

In Figure A-1 we use the conventional Δ to represent change in a variable: $\Delta y = y_2 - y_1$ and $\Delta x = x_2 - x_1$. To assure ourselves that b is indeed the slope of the line drawn representing the linear function (see Figure A-1), let x take on specific values x_1 and x_2 and calculate the corresponding y values, y_1 and y_2.

$$y_1 = a + bx_1 \qquad (A.2)$$

$$y_2 = a + bx_2 \qquad (A.3)$$

Subtracting equation (A.3) from equation (A.2) gives

$$y_2 - y_1 = b(x_2 - x_1) \qquad (A.4)$$

$$\Delta y = b\Delta x \qquad (A.5)$$

or $$\frac{\Delta y}{\Delta x} = b \qquad (A.6)$$

The ratio $\Delta y/\Delta x$ shows that b represents what we would like the slope to represent: the change in y associated with a change in x. This ratio, which we will use a great deal in what follows, is often called the *incremental ratio*. Since equation (A.6) is true for any pair of x values and corresponding y values, we can see that the slope of a linear function at any point is a constant. This property of linear functions makes their analysis relatively simple. Nonlinear functions do not possess this property, as examination of Figure A-2 will show.

The line drawn connecting the points (α, β) on the curve is called a *chord*. The slope of a chord joining any two points on a curve is always equal to the incremental ratio of the function graphed for the pair of points in question. Thus, both the incremental ratio and the slope of the chord joining any two points on a curve can be considered a linear approximation of the change in the function. The differential calculus is a method of determining rates of change of functions which are not necessarily linear. We can see

---

[1] The assignment of labels independent and dependent to variables in mathematics is purely arbitrary and does not constitute a causal assumption. We can rewrite equation (A.1) with x as dependent,

$$x = (y - a)/b$$

without changing the meaning of the mathematical statement. By convention, the variable on the left-hand side is called dependent.

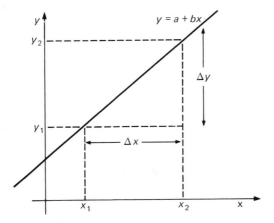

Figure A-1. Graph of a Linear Function.

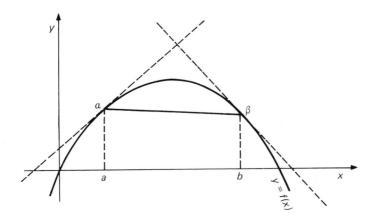

Figure A-2. Slopes at Two Points of a Non-Linear Function.

that what we wish to determine is the slope of the line tangent to the curve at the point in question. That is, to express the change in y associated with change in any particular x value (as we might ask how does status change when we vary education in its upper range) of a nonlinear function we must find a way to measure the slope of the tangent to the curve $y = f(x)$ at the point x_0 in question.

It is clear that the incremental ratio or the slope of the chord joining any point on a curve with any other point depends on the second point chosen.

This ratio varies as the second point chosen varies. As we move the point *b* to the left and to the right on the *x* coordinate in Figure A-2 the incremental ratio of the points (*α, β*) varies as *β* varies. Thus the incremental ratio will not serve in general as a measure of changes in a dependent variable associated with changes in an independent variable.

In Figure A-2, $\Delta x = b - a$. Imagine moving the point *b* closer and closer to the point *a*. We can see that the slope of the chord comes closer and closer to the slope of the tangent as Δx becomes very small. (See Figure A-3.) More abstractly, we can say that as $\Delta x \to 0$ (read "as *x* approaches zero"),

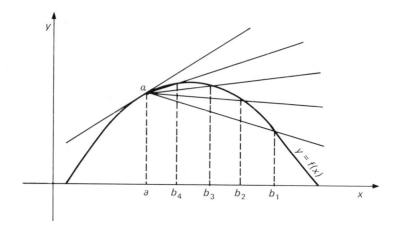

Figure A-3. Slope as Limit of Slope of Chords.

$\Delta y/\Delta x \to dy/dx$, where *dy/dx* denotes the slope of the tangent. The latter quantity plays a central role in the differential calculus and is called the *derivative*. The derivative of a function is a function (a derived function) which when it exists provides a unique measure of the rate of change of a function at any point.[2] In particular it shows the slope of the curve representing the original function at any point selected.

---

[2] Derivatives exist only for *continuous* functions. Mathematicians are usually concerned with what is called *point continuity* which is defined technically as follows: A function $y = f(x)$ is continuous at a point *a*, if $f(a)$ exists, i.e., the function is defined at *a*, the limit of the function as *x* approaches *a* must exist and must be equal to $f(a)$, i.e.,

$$\lim_{x \to a} f(x) \text{ exists} \quad \text{and} \quad \lim_{x \to a} f(x) = f(a)$$

To understand derivatives we must consider at a very intuitive level the very important mathematical concept of a *limit*. Above we suggested that we could make $\Delta y/\Delta x$ close to dy/dx as we made x smaller and smaller. In fact, it turns out that we can make $\Delta y/\Delta x$ as close to dy/dx as we want. To understand how this is possible, consider as an example the function $1/x$ or $(y = f(x) = 1/x)$. As x increases, the value of the function gets smaller and smaller. While we can never make the value of the function zero (since division by zero is not defined), we can make it very close to zero. We can express this by saying we can make $1/x$ smaller than any real number one might choose by making x sufficiently large. We say that the value of the function $1/x$ approaches the limit zero (or in the limit approaches zero) as x approaches infinity. Symbolically:

$$\lim_{x \to \infty} \left(\frac{1}{x} \right) = 0 \qquad (A.7)$$

More abstractly, let ε denote any small number greater than 0. In general, we say that the function $1/x$ approaches a *finite limit* L as x approaches infinity, if for *any* ε there is some x large enough that $L - f(x) < \varepsilon$. In other words, no matter how small the ε, we can choose an x so that this difference is less than ε.

In similar fashion, we can evaluate the limit of a function as $x \to 0$. We can say that for any $\varepsilon > 0$, no matter how small, we can choose an x value small enough so that $L - f(x) < \varepsilon$. We can say that $L - f(x)$ becomes and remains less than any nonzero number, no matter how small, as x decreases to zero.

Thus, we can write our assertion that the value of the incremental ratio approaches the slope of the tangent to the curve, as Δx gets smaller and smaller, as follows:

$$\lim_{\Delta x \to 0} \left(\frac{\Delta y}{\Delta x} \right) = \frac{dy}{dx} \qquad (A.8)$$

We can summarize in a few sentences what we now know about the derivative.

1. The derivative of a function at any point, for which it is defined, is the slope of the tangent to the curve at that point.
2. We interpret the derivative as indicating how y changes, as x changes, at the point at which the derivative is evaluated.
3. The slope of the chord joining the points x_1 and y_1 and $(x_1 + \Delta x_1, y_1 + \Delta y_1)$ gets closer and closer to the slope of the tangent at (x_1, y_1) as Δx is made smaller and smaller.

4. The derivative, which represents the *instantaneous rate of change* of a function at a given point, is a limiting abstract concept.

In line with this last statement, Allen notes: "The mathematically significant fact is that a function is *tending* to increase at a certain rate at a definite point, not that it *actually* increases at a certain average rate over a definite range of the variable" [Allen 1938, p. 135].

The next step, which comprises the bulk of the differential calculus, is to find an analytical method for finding the slope of the tangent, dy/dx. Most treatments denote the change in x in the incremental ratio as h instead of as Δx. Then the change in y (or Δy) is equal to the new value of the function $f(x)$, after x takes on a new value *minus* the old value. Thus

$$\frac{dy}{dx} = \lim_{\Delta x \to 0} \left(\frac{\Delta y}{\Delta x}\right) = \lim_{h \to 0} \frac{f(x + h) - f(x)}{h} \tag{A.9}$$

Since we are evaluating the function $f(x)$ we may also write

$$\frac{d}{dx} f(x) = f'(x) = \lim_{h \to 0} \frac{f(x + h) - f(x)}{h} \tag{A.10}$$

We can use this formula to derive all of the tools necessary to calculate derivatives of complicated expressions. Several examples might prove helpful.

(i) If $f(x) = c$, where c is constant,

$$\lim_{h \to 0} \frac{f(x + h) - f(x)}{h} = \lim_{h \to 0} \frac{a - a}{h} = 0 \tag{A.11}$$

Thus the derivative of a constant is always equal to zero.

(ii) If $y = f(x) = x^2$,

$$\lim_{h \to 0} \frac{f(x + h) - f(x)}{h} = \lim_{h \to 0} \frac{(x + h)^2 - x^2}{h}$$

$$= \lim_{h \to 0} \frac{x^2 - 2xh + h^2 - x^2}{h} \tag{A.12}$$

$$= \lim_{h \to 0} \frac{2xh + h^2}{h} = 2x$$

In fact, one of the important general results we can prove (but will not here) is that if $f(x)$ is a power function,

$$y = ax^n \tag{A.13}$$

$$\frac{dy}{dx} = nax^{n-1} \tag{A.14}$$

Another point we must consider is the function-of-function or *chain rule*. If we have a function of a function

$$y = y(z) \tag{A.15}$$

$$z = z(x) \tag{A.16}$$

and wish to find dy/dx, we can use the following rule:

$$\frac{dy}{dx} = \frac{dy}{dz}\frac{dz}{dx} \tag{A.17}$$

We use this result quite often in Chapter 2.

Finally, we can take the derivative of a derivative (which is, recall, a function in its own right). We call this the second derivative and denote it by the following notation:

$$\frac{d^2y}{dx^2} = f''(x) \tag{A.18}$$

Similarly, we can define a third derivative, a fourth derivative, and so on, to an nth derivative, denoted as follows:

$$\frac{d^3y}{dx^3} = f'''(x)$$
$$\vdots \qquad \vdots \tag{A.19}$$
$$\frac{d^ny}{dx^n} = f^{(n)}(x)$$

The second derivative measures the instantaneous rate of change of the first derivative at a given point. For example, a speedometer reading gives us the first derivative of a function relating distance to time. The second derivative of this function gives us what we call acceleration. It would be highly unlikely that social scientists would use derivatives of order higher than two.

To this point we have restricted our attention to functions of one variable (bivariate relations). The reader is well aware of the fact that sociologists are seldom willing or even able to restrict their analyses to bivariate relations. Say, for example, we have a function of the following form,

$$y = 10x^2 + 2x^4z^{-2} - 3z^3 \tag{A.20}$$

and we want to find the derivative of the function holding one of the independent variables constant. We will find that this is possible and that if we hold z, say, constant we can proceed as above in evaluating the derivative of a function of a single variable. That is we imagine the function to be of the form

$$y = 10x^2 + 2ax^4 - c \tag{A.21}$$

where

$$a = z^{-2} \quad \text{and} \quad -3z^{-3} = c$$

Thus, when we differentiate (term by term), we obtain a value of

$$20x + 8cx^3z^{-2} \tag{A.22}$$

for the derivative using the rules formulated in (A.11) and (A.12 and A.13) above.

To acknowledge the fact that when we take the derivative of a function of two or more variables, we must hold all but one of the independent variables constant to speak of *partial derivatives* or just "partials." Partial derivatives are generally denoted by deltas instead of Roman d's. Thus, from equation (A.20) we have

$$\frac{\partial y}{\partial x} = 20x + 8x^3z^{-2} \tag{A.23}$$

$$\frac{\partial y}{\partial z} = -4x^4z^{-3} - 9z^2 \tag{A.24}$$

Partials are also denoted

$$fx = \frac{\partial y}{\partial x} = \frac{\partial f(x, z)}{\partial x} \tag{A.25}$$

$$fz = \frac{\partial y}{\partial z} = \frac{\partial f(x, z)}{\partial z} \tag{A.26}$$

All three expressions in (A.25) are read "the partial derivative of y with respect to x."

Following our earlier development, we can give a formal definition of partial derivatives. Consider the general function $y = f(x, z)$. The partial derivative of y with respect to x is defined as follows:

$$\frac{\partial y}{\partial x} = \lim_{\Delta x \to 0} \frac{f(x + \Delta x, z) - f(x, z)}{\Delta x}$$

$$= \lim_{h \to 0} \frac{f(x + h; z) - f(x, z)}{h} \tag{A.27}$$

and the partial of y with respect to z is defined as follows:

$$\frac{\partial y}{\partial z} = \lim_{\Delta x \to 0} \frac{f(x; z + \Delta z) - f(x, z)}{\Delta x}$$

$$= \lim_{h \to 0} \frac{f(x; z + h) - f(x, z)}{h} \tag{A.28}$$

Notice that the solution (A.22) to equation (A.20) with which we began, $\partial y/\partial x$, is a function not only of x but also of z. The partial derivative can in general be given a specific value when the values of the independent variable(s) held constant are given values. The fact that $\partial y/\partial x$ depends not only on x but also on z suggests that we consider what happens to $\partial y/\partial x$ (the reaction of y to x) as z changes:

$$\frac{\partial\left(\frac{\partial y}{\partial x}\right)}{\partial z} \tag{A.29}$$

This expresses in formal terms the question "how does responsiveness of y to a change in x vary as z varies?"

Applying this to equation (A.23), yields

$$\frac{\partial\left(\frac{\partial y}{\partial z}\right)}{\partial x} = -16x^3z^{-3} \tag{A.30}$$

Similarly

$$\frac{\partial\left(\frac{\partial y}{\partial x}\right)}{\partial z} = -16x^3z^{-3} \tag{A.31}$$

The following are common notational variations:

$$\frac{\partial\left(\frac{\partial y}{\partial x}\right)}{\partial z} = \frac{\partial^2 y}{\partial x \partial z} = \int_{xz} \tag{A.32}$$

The third expression indicates that the function has been differentiated first with respect to x and then with respect to z. These terms are all referred to as *second-order cross-partial derivatives* or "cross-partials." In the example we computed, we found that $\int_{xz} = \int_{zx}$. This is always true for any function $f(x, z)$.

A related question which sometimes arises is "what happens to $\partial y/\partial x$ as x changes?" Answering this question involves a straightforward extension of previous results. We merely differentiate equation (A.23) again.

$$\frac{\partial\left(\frac{\partial y}{\partial x}\right)}{\partial x} = 20 + 24x^2z^{-2} \tag{A.33}$$

The following are extensions of our notation:

$$\frac{\partial\left(\frac{\partial y}{\partial x}\right)}{\partial x} = \frac{\partial^2 y}{\partial x^2} = \int xx \tag{A.34}$$

All of these symbols represent the *second-order partial derivative* of y with respect to x.

We can now summarize the points we have considered regarding the partial derivatives of the function $y = f(x, z)$.

1.   There are two first-order partial derivatives of a differentiable function in three variables, $y = f(x, z)$, written $\int x$ and $\int z$ or $\partial y/\partial x$ and $\partial y/\partial z$. They are obtained by differentiating the function with respect to the relevant variable holding the others constant.

2.   There are two equal second-order cross-partial derivatives $\int xz$ and $\int zx$. They are obtained by differentiating $f(x, z)$ first with respect to x and then with respect to z in the first case, and the reverse in the second.

3.   There are two direct second-order partial derivatives $\int xx$ and $\int zz$. These are obtained by differentiating $f(x, z)$ twice with respect to x, in the first case, and with respect to z, in the second case.

This discussion has been extremely brief and incomplete. It seems to be very helpful, generally, in attempting to understand partial derivatives to study their geometrical interpretation. The reader is urged to do this. To this end, we particularly recommend the book by Archibald and Lipsey [1967].

There is another very important way in which we can express change in a dependent variable as a function of changes in independent variables. Let's begin with the same function $y = f(x, z)$ and address the question how does y vary when *both* x and z vary. That is, we are seeking $\Delta y = f(\Delta x, \Delta z)$ We can represent this change as follows:

$$\Delta y = f(x + \Delta x; z + \Delta z) - f(x, z) \tag{A.35}$$

This says that if x increases by Δx and z increases by Δz, the change in y is found by discovering the value of y when the new values of x and z are inserted into the function and subtracting the old value of the function. Following Archibald and Lipsey [1967], we perform a few algebraic manipulations to achieve the desired result. First, we add and subtract $f(x, z + \Delta z)$ to the right-hand side of equation (A.35), so that (A.35) becomes

$$\Delta y = f(x + \Delta x; z + \Delta z) - f(x; z + \Delta z) + f(x; z + \Delta z) - f(x, z) \tag{A.36}$$

Next, we multiply the first two terms on the right-hand side of equation

(A.36) by $\Delta x/\Delta x$, and the last two terms by $\Delta z/\Delta z$. These manipulations give us

$$\Delta y = \frac{[f(x + \Delta x; z + \Delta z) - f(x; z + \Delta z)]\Delta x}{\Delta x}$$

$$+ \frac{[f(x; z + \Delta z) - f(x, z)]\Delta z}{\Delta z} \qquad (A.37)$$

We now have Δy as the sum of two terms, the first a ratio of a complicated expression to the change in x, and the second, a ratio of a complicated expression to the change in z.

Now we proceed as we did with simple derivatives; we try to find the limit of these two ratios as the changes in x and z get smaller and smaller, i.e., as $\Delta x \to 0$ and $\Delta z \to 0$. We ignore for the present the change terms Δx and Δz in the numerators of these ratios. Let's consider the first term. We want to find

$$\lim_{\Delta x \to 0} \frac{f(x + \Delta x; z + \Delta z) - f(x; z + \Delta z)}{\Delta x} \qquad (A.38)$$

Referring back to the definition of a partial derivative, we can see that this is the partial derivative of y with respect to x evaluated at the point $(x; z + \Delta z)$. Thus (A.38) is

$$\frac{\partial}{\partial x} f(x; z + \Delta z) = \int x \qquad (A.39)$$

As Δx approaches zero this will approach $\int x$ evaluated at the point (x, z).

Similarly, for the second term in equation (A.37) we wish to find

$$\lim_{\Delta z \to 0} \frac{f(x; z + \Delta z) - f(x, z)}{\Delta z} \qquad (A.40)$$

Again, we find that (A.40) is the partial derivative of y with respect to z, evaluated at the point (x, z).

$$\frac{\partial}{\partial z} f(x, y) = \int z \qquad (A.41)$$

We have now taken the limits of both terms on the right-hand side of equation (A.37). Replacing the terms Δx and Δz, which we have ignored to this point, we see that

$$\lim_{\substack{\Delta x \to 0 \\ \Delta z \to 0}} \Delta y = \int x\Delta x + \int z\Delta z \qquad (A.42)$$

Equation (A.42) gives an approximation to the correct value of Δy as x and z change together, the approximation becoming better and better as Δx and Δz get closer and closer to zero. Thus we can write

$$\Delta y = \int x\Delta x + \int z\Delta z + \varepsilon \tag{A.43}$$

where ε is an error term that can be made as small as desired by taking Δx and Δz appropriately close to zero. In order to indicate that we are concerned with arbitrarily small increments in x and z, not just increments of any magnitude, we write dy in place of Δy, dx in place of Δx, and dz in place of Δz. This defines the *total differential* of the function.

$$dy = \int x\,dx + \int z\,dz \tag{A.44}$$

Using the alternate notation for partial derivatives, this is written as follows:

$$dy = \frac{\partial y}{\partial x}\,dx + \frac{\partial y}{\partial z}\,dz \tag{A.45}$$

This a very important result in that it tells us that we may use the partial derivatives of a function with respect to each of its arguments (the independent variables), multiplied by the small change in each of the corresponding independent variables, and sum the result, even though each partial was evaluated holding all of the other independent variables constant. It tells us that this approximation will not result in much error, if the changes in all of the independent variables are small.

First, we apply this strategy to the function of a single-variable case, i.e., where $y = f(x)$. We can approximate the change in y, in response race change in x, as follows:

$$dy = f'(x)\,dx \tag{A.46}$$

If we evaluate $f'(x)$ at any point, we obtain the slope of the tangent to the curve at that point. Thus, equation (A.46) is a linear function relating dy to dx by a constant, the slope of the tangent to that point. Figure A-4 should help illustrate this point.

The reader can see that when we use equation (A.46) to estimate dy for a given dx, we are estimating dy by moving along the tangent (T), instead of moving along the curve representing the function. This procedure clearly produces some error of estimation, which in Figure A-4 is labeled ε. As we would expect from the development to this point (and as should be obvious from inspection of Figure A-4), as $dx \to 0$ the error $\varepsilon \to 0$.

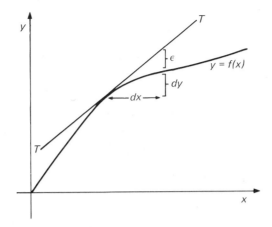

Figure A–4. Error in Extrapolation From the Slope at a Point.

In the three-variable case, the total differential moves along the plane that is tangent to the surface, formed by the variables of concern at the point Q at which the differential is evaluated. This is illustrated in Figure A-5. Measuring changes in y according to equation (A.44) involves moving along this tangent plane when the surface is likely to be curved. But again, the error may be as small as desired by making dx and dz appropriately small.

There are four points to be made in summarizing the basic result on differentials.

1. There is only one way in which a function of a single variable can change, and that is as a result of changes in the independent variable. The variation of the function in that case is then adequately described by the derivative. It is more complicated, however, to express changes in a function of two or more variables. We have seen that we can express such changes by means of the total differential.

2. We have seen that when the independent variables in the function $y = f(x, z)$ vary together, we can express changes in y as follows:

$$dy = \frac{\partial y}{\partial x}\, dx + \frac{\partial y}{\partial z}\, dz$$

3. The above result depended on our considering small increments in the independent variables. These arbitrarily small increments are often called *differentials* and since the derivative may be regarded as a ratio of two differentials, it is sometimes called the "differential coefficient."

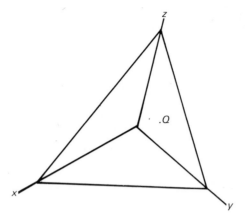

Figure A-5. Plane in Three Dimensional Space.

4. The extension to functions of n variables is straightforward. If $y = f(x_1, x_2, \ldots, x_n)$ we can express the change in y as follows:

$$dy = \frac{\partial y}{\partial x_1} dx_1 + \frac{\partial y}{\partial x_2} dx_2 + \cdots + \frac{\partial y}{\partial x_n} dx_n \qquad (A.47)$$

All that remains to be demonstrated for the results of Chapter 2 is that the expression of the total differential holds whether the variables on the right hand side are independent (assumed to this point) or are themselves functions. That is, we must apply the "chain rule" to the formula for the total differential.

It can be shown that if $y = f(x, z)$ and $x = x(t)$ and $z = z(t)$, that

$$\frac{dy}{dt} = \frac{\partial y}{\partial x}\frac{dx}{dt} + \frac{\partial y}{\partial z}\frac{dz}{dt} \qquad (A.48)$$

and more generally if $y = f(x_1, \ldots, x_n)$ and $x_1 = f_1(t), \ldots, x_n = f_n(t)$,

$$\frac{dy}{dt} = \frac{\partial y}{\partial x_1}\frac{dx_1}{dt} + \cdots + \frac{\partial y}{\partial x_n}\frac{dx_n}{dt} \qquad (A.49)$$

Secondly, if $y = f(x, z)$ and $z = g(x)$, i.e., that one of the arguments of the function $f(x, z)$ is a function of the other argument, we can show

$$\frac{dy}{dx} = \frac{\partial y}{\partial x} + \frac{\partial y}{\partial x}\frac{dz}{dx} \qquad (A.50)$$

Similarly, if $y = f(x, z)$ and $x = h(z)$,

$$\frac{dy}{dz} = \frac{\partial y}{\partial x}\frac{dx}{dz} + \frac{dy}{dz} \tag{A.51}$$

A third case is the one in which $y = f(x,z)$, $x = g(u, v)$ and $z = h(u, v)$. We can obtain an expression showing changes in y as a function of changes in u and v.

$$dy = \frac{\partial y}{\partial x}\,dx + \frac{\partial y}{\partial z}\,dz \tag{A.52}$$

$$dx = \frac{\partial x}{\partial u}\,du + \frac{\partial x}{\partial v}\,dv \tag{A.53}$$

$$dz = \frac{\partial z}{\partial u}\,du + \frac{\partial z}{\partial v}\,dv \tag{A.54}$$

or

$$dy = \frac{\partial y}{\partial x}\left(\frac{\partial x}{\partial u}\,du + \frac{\partial x}{\partial v}\,dv\right) + \frac{\partial y}{\partial z}\left(\frac{\partial z}{\partial u}\,du + \frac{\partial z}{\partial v}\,dv\right) \tag{A.55}$$

and by rearranging for du and dv, we obtain

$$dy = \left(\frac{\partial y}{\partial x}\frac{\partial x}{\partial u} + \frac{\partial y}{\partial z}\frac{\partial z}{\partial u}\right)du + \left(\frac{\partial y}{\partial x}\frac{\partial x}{\partial v} + \frac{\partial y}{\partial z}\frac{\partial z}{\partial v}\right)dv \tag{A.56}$$

Now we can take the partial derivative of y with respect to u, and since dv would be held constant (and be, accordingly, zero), we obtain

$$\frac{\partial y}{\partial u} = \frac{\partial y}{\partial x}\frac{\partial x}{\partial u} + \frac{\partial y}{\partial z}\frac{\partial z}{\partial u} \tag{A.57}$$

Similarly, the partial of y with respect to v is obtained as follows:

$$\frac{\partial y}{\partial v} = \frac{\partial y}{\partial x}\frac{\partial x}{\partial v} + \frac{\partial y}{\partial z}\frac{\partial z}{\partial v} \tag{A.58}$$

Finally, we can obtain the differential of a partial derivative. Since, as we have noted earlier, a partial derivative of the function $f(x, z)$ is a function of both independent variables, we may apply the above results to obtain

$$d\frac{\partial y}{\partial x} = \frac{\partial}{\partial x}\frac{\partial y}{\partial x}\,dx + \frac{\partial}{\partial z}\frac{\partial y}{\partial x}\,dz = \frac{\partial^2 y}{\partial x^2}\,dx + \frac{\partial^2}{\partial x\,\partial z}\,dz \tag{A.59}$$

and

$$d \frac{\partial y}{\partial z} = \frac{\partial}{\partial x} \frac{\partial y}{\partial z} dx + \frac{\partial}{\partial z} \frac{\partial y}{\partial z} dz = \frac{\partial^2 y}{\partial x \partial z} dz + \frac{\partial^2 y}{\partial z^2} dz \qquad (A.60)$$

This concludes the presentation of the results necessary for an understanding of the theorems presented in Chapter 2. Obviously the reader who is encountering these results for the first time will not be able to grasp the meaning of the specific results, particularly those just presented, on first reading. This presentation provides all of the materials needed for this dissertation but leaves a great deal unsaid regarding the mathematics involved.

References

Aiken, Michael, and Hage, Jerald.
 1968. "Organizational Interdependence and Interorganizational Structure." *American Sociological Review* 33 (December): 912–931.

Alker, Hayward R., Jr.
 1969. "A Typology of Ecological Fallacies." In *Quantitative Ecological Analysis in the Social Sciences*. Edited by M. Dogan and S. Rokkan. Cambridge, Mass.: MIT Press. Pp. 69–86.

Allardt, Erik.
 1969. "Aggregate Analysis: The Problem of Its Informative Value." In *Quantitative Ecological Analysis in the Social Sciences*. Edited by M. Dogan and S. Rokkan. Cambridge, Mass.: MIT Press. Pp. 41–52.

Allen, R. G. D.
 1938. *Mathematical Analysis for Economists*. London: Macmillan.
 1956. *Mathematical Economics*. London: Macmillan.

Almond, Gabriel, and Verba, Sidney.
 1963. *The Civic Culture*. Princeton: Princeton University Press.

Ando, A.; Fisher, F. M.; and Simon, H. A.
 1963. *Essays on the Structure of Social Science Models*. Cambridge, Mass.: MIT Press.

Archibald, G. C., and Lipsey, C. G.
 1967. *An Introduction to a Mathematical Treatment of Economics*. London: Weidenfeld and Nicholson.

Blalock, Hubert M.
 1961. "Correlated Independent Variables: The Problem of Multicollinearity." *Social Forces* 42 (December): 233–237.
 1964. *Causal Inferences in Nonexperimental Research*. Chapel Hill: University of North Carolina Press.
 1966. "The Identification Problem and Theory Building: The Case of Status Inconsistency." *American Sociological Review* 31 (February): 34–47.
 1967. *Toward a Theory of Minority-Group Relations*. New York: Wiley.
 1968. "Theory Building and Causal Inferences." In *Methodology in Social Research*. Edited by H. M. Blalock and Ann Blalock. New York: McGraw-Hill. Pp. 155–198.
 1971. "Aggregation and Measurement Error." Unpublished Paper.

Blau, Peter M.
    1960. "Structural Effects." *American Sociological Review* 25 (April): 178–192.

Blau, Peter M., and Duncan, O. Dudley.
    1967. *The American Occupational Structure*. New York: Wiley.

Boot, J. C. G., and deWit, G. M.
    1960. "Investment Demand: An Empirical Contribution to the Aggregation Problem." *International Economic Review* 1 (January): 3–30.

Boudon, Raymond.
    1963. "Propriétés Individuelles et Propriétés Collectives: Une Probleme d'Analyse Ecologique." *Revue Francaise de Sociologie* 4 (July-September): 275–299.

Brown, T. Merritt.
    1970. *The Specification and Uses of Econometric Models*. London: Macmillan.

Campbell, E., and Alexander, C. Norman.
    1965. "Structural Effects and Interpersonal Relationships." *American Journal of Sociology* 71 (November): 284–289.

Casetti, Emilio.
    1966. "Analysis of Spatial Association by Trigonometric Polynomials." *Canadian Geographer* 10, No. 4: 199–204.

Christ, Carl.
    1966. *Econometric Models and Methods*. New York: Wiley.

Coleman, James S.
    1958–
    1959. "Relational Analysis: The Study of Social Organization with Survey Methods." *Human Organization* 17 (Winter): 28–36.
    1964. *Introduction to Mathematical Sociology*. Glencoe, Ill.: The Free Press.

Cramer, J. S.
    1964. "Efficient Grouping: Regression and Correlation in Engel Curve Analysis." *Journal of the American Statistical Association* 59 (March): 233–250.

Curry, Leslie.
    1966. "A Note on Spatial Association." *The Professional Geographer* 18 (March): 97–99.
    1967. "Quantitative Geography, 1967." *The Canadian Geographer* 11, No. 4: 265–279.

Davis, James A.
1959. "A Formal Interpretation of the Theory of Relative Deprivation."
Sociometry 22 (December): 280–296.

Davis, James; Spaeth, J.; and Huson, C.
1961. "Analysing the Effects of Group Composition." *American Sociological Review* 26 (April): 215–225.

Dogan, Mattei, and Rokkan, Stein, eds.
1969. *Quantitative Ecological Analysis in the Social Sciences.* Cambridge, Mass.: MIT Press.

Duncan, Otis Dudley, and Davis, Beverly.
1953. "An Alternative to Ecological Correlation." *American Sociological Review* 18 (December): 665–666.

Duncan, Otis Dudley; Cuzzort, Ray P.; and Duncan Beverly, D.
1961. *Statistical Geography.* Glencoe, Ill.: Free Press.

Fennessey, James.
1968. "The General Linear Model: A Perspective on Some Familiar Topics." *American Journal of Sociology* 74 (July): 1–27.

Fisher, Franklin M.
1969. "Approximate Aggregation and Leontief Conditions." *Econometrica* 37 (July): 457–469.

Fisher, Walter D.
1962. "Optimal Aggregation in Multi-Equation Prediction Models." *Econometrica* 30 (October): 744–769.
1969. *Clustering and Aggregation in Economics.* Baltimore: Johns Hopkins University Press.

Fishman, George S.
1969. *Spectral Methods in Econometrics.* Cambridge, Mass.: Harvard University Press.

Fleisher, Belton M.
1966. *The Economics of Delinquency.* Chicago: Quadrangle.

Fox, Karl.
1968. *Intermediate Economic Statistics.* New York: Wiley.

Freund, John E.
1962. *Mathematical Statistics.* Englewood Cliffs, N.J.: Prentice Hall.

Frisch, R.
1934. *Statistical Confluence Analysis by Means of Complete Regression Systems.* Oslo: University Economics Institute.

136

Galtung, Johan.
  1967. *Theory and Methods of Social Research.* New York: Columbia University Press.

Gehkle, C., and Biehel, R.
  1934. "Certain Effects of Grouping upon the Size of the Correlation Coefficient in Census Tract Material," *Journal of the American Statistical Association Supplement* 29: 169–170.

Goldberger, Arthur S.
  1964. *Econometric Theory.* New York: Wiley.
  1968. *Topics in Regression Analysis.* New York: Macmillan.

Goodman, Leo.
  1953. "Ecological Regression and the Behavior of Individuals." *American Journal of Sociology* 64 (May): 610–625.
  1959. "Some Alternatives to Ecological Correlation." *American Journal of Sociology* 64 (May): 610–625.

Gordon, Robert.
  1968. "Issues in Multiple Regression." *American Journal of Sociology* 73 (March): 592–616.

Green, H. A. John.
  1964. *Aggregation in Economic Analysis.* Princeton: Princeton University Press.

Grunfeld, Yehuda, and Griliches, Zvi.
  1960. "Is Aggregation Necessarily Bad?" *Review of Economics and Statistics* 42 (February): 1–13.

Gupta, K. L.
  1969. *Aggregation in Economics: A Theoretical and Empirical Study.* Rotterdam: Rotterdam University Press.

Hannan, Michael T.
  1970a. *Problems of Aggregation and Disaggregation in Sociological Research.* Chapel Hill, N.C.: Institute for Research in the Social Sciences: Methodology Working Paper #4.
  1970b. "Aggregation and Structural Measurement." Paper read at American Sociological Association Meetings.
  1971. "Problems of Aggregation." In *Causal Models in the Social Sciences.* Edited by Hubert M. Blalock. Chicago: Aldine.

Hauser, Robert M.
  1969. "Schools and the Stratification Process." *American Journal of Sociology* 74 (May): 587–611.

Hildreth, C., and Houck, J. P.
    1968. "Some Estimators for a Linear Model with Random Coefficients."
    Journal of the American Statistical Association 63 (June):
    584–595.

Hoffman, Stephen.
    1970. *Advanced Calculus.* Englewood Cliffs, N.J.: Prentice Hall.

Homans, George C.
    1961. *Social Behavior: Its Elementary Forms.* New York: Harcourt,
    Brace and World.

Johnston, J.
    1963. *Econometric Methods.* New York: McGraw-Hill.

Keynes, John Maynard.
    1936. *The General Theory of Employment, Interest, and Money.* New
    York: Harcourt, Brace and Co.

Klein, Lawrence R.
    1946. "Remarks on the Theory of Aggregation." *Econometrica* 14
    (October): 303–312.
    1953. *A Textbook of Econometrics.* Evanston, Ill.: Row, Peterson.

Kmenta, Jan.
    1971. *Elements of Econometrics.* New York: Macmillan.

Kooros, A.
    1965. *Elements of Mathematical Economics.* Boston: Houghton Mifflin.

Lancaster, Kelvin.
    1966. "Economic Aggregation and Additivity." In *The Structure of
    Economic Science: Essays on Methodology.* Edited by Sherman
    Krupp. Englewood Cliffs, N.J.: Prentice Hall. Pp. 201–215.

Larzarsfeld, Paul, and Menzel, Herbert.
    1965. "On the Relations between Individual and Collective Properties."
    In *Complex Organizations.* Edited by Amitai Etzioni. New
    York: Holt, Rinehart and Winston. Pp. 422–440.

Leontief, W. W.
    1947a. "A Note on the Interrelation of Subsets of Independent
    Variables of a Continuous Function with Continuous First
    Derivatives." *Bulletli of the American Mathematical Society* 53:
    343–350.
    1947b. "Introduction to a Theory of Internal Structure of Functional
    Relationships." *Econometrica* 15 (October): 361–373.

Linz, Juan J.
   1969. "Ecological Analysis and Survey Research." In *Quantitative Ecological Analysis in the Social Sciences.* Edited by M. Dogan and S. Rokkan. Cambridge, Mass.: MIT Press. Pp. 91–132.

Lipset, Seymour; Trow, Martin; and Coleman, James.
   1956. *Union Democracy.* Glencoe, Ill.: Free Press.

McFarland, David D.
   1970. "Intergenerational Social Mobility as a Markov Process: Including a Time-Stationary Markovian Model That Explains Declines in Mobility Rates." *American Sociological Review* 35 (June): 463–475.

Malinvaud, E.
   1966. *Statistical Methods of Econometrics.* Chicago: Rand McNally.

May, Kenneth O.
   1946. "The Aggregation Problem for a One-Industry Model." *Econometrica* 14 (October): 285–298.

Menzel, H., and Katz, E.
   1966. "Social Relations and Innovation in the Medical Profession." *Public Opinion Quarterly* 19 (Winter): 337–352.

Merritt, Richard L., and Rokkan, Stein, eds.
   1966. *Comparing Nations: The Uses of Quantitative Data.* New Haven: Yale University Press.

Nataf, Andre.
   1948. "Sur la Possibilité de Construction de Certains Macromodèles." *Econometrica* 16 (July): 232–244.
   1960. "Résults et Directions de Recherche dans la Théorie de l'Aggrégation." In *Logic, Methodology and Philosophy of Science.* Edited by E. Nagal, P. Suppes, and A. Tarski. Stanford, Calif.: Stanford University Press.
   1968. "Aggregation." In *International Encyclopedia of the Social Sciences.* Edited by D. Sills. New York: Macmillan and The Free Press. Pp. 162–168.

Parsons, Talcott.
   1956. "The Relation Between the Small Group and the Larger Social System." In *Toward a Unified Theory of Behavior.* Edited by Roy Grinkler. New York: Basic Books. Pp 190–200.

Peston, M. H.
   1959. "A View of the Aggregation Problem." *The Review of Economic Studies* 27 (October): 58–64.

Price, Hugh S.
  1968. "Micro- and Macro-Politics: Notes on Research Strategy." In *Political Research and Political Theory.* Editer by Oliver Garceau. Cambridge, Mass.: Harvard University Press. Pp. 102–140.

Pu, Shou Shan.
  1946. "A Note on Macroeconomics." *Econometrica* 14 (October): 299–302.

Quirk, James, and Saposnik, Rubin.
  1968. *Introduction to General Equilibrium Theory and Welfare Economics.* New York: McGraw-Hill.

Riley, Matilda White.
  1963. *Sociological Research.* New York: Harcourt, Brace and World.

Robinson, A. H.
  1956. "The Necessity of Weighting Values in Correlation Analysis of Areal Data." *Annals of the Association of American Geographers* 46 (March): 233–236.

Robinson, William S.
  1950. "Ecological Correlations and the Behavior of Individuals." *American Sociological Review* 15 (June): 351–357.

Rokkan, Stein.
  1962. "The Comparative Study of Political Participation: Notes Toward a Perspective on Current Research." In *Essays on the Behavioral Study of Politics.* Edited by A. Ranney. Urbana: University of Illinois Press. Pp. 47–90.

Ryder, Norman.
  1965. "The Cohort in the Study of Social Change." *American Sociological Review* 30 (December): 843–861.

Scheuch, Erwin K.
  1969. "Social Context and Individual Behavior." In *Quantitative Ecological Analysis in the Social Sciences.* Edited by M. Dogan and S. Rokkan. Cambridge, Mass.: MIT Press. Pp 133–156.

Schuessler, Karl.
  1969. "Covariance Analysis in Sociological Research." In *Sociological Methodology* 1969. Edited by E. Borgotta and G. Bohrenstedt. San Francisco: Josey Bass. Pp. 219–244.

Selvin, Hanan E.
  1958. "Durkheim's 'Suicide' and Problems of Empirical Research." *American Journal of Sociology* 63 (May): 607–619.

Shively, W. Phillips.
    1969. " 'Ecological' Inference: The Use of Aggregate Data to Study Individuals." *American Political Science Review* 63 (December): 1183–1196.

Simon, Julian L.
    1968. "The Effect of Income on Suicide Rate: A Paradox Resolved," *American Journal of Sociology* 74 (November): 302–303.

Slatin, Gerald T.
    1969. "Ecological Analysis of Delinquency." *American Sociological Review* 34 (December): 894–906.

Sprout, Harold, and Sprout, Margaret.
    1965. *The Ecological Perspective on Human Affairs: With Special Reference to International Politics.* Princeton: Princeton University Press.

Stokes, Donald.
    1969. "Cross-Level Inference as a Game Against Nature." In *Mathematical Applications in Political Science IV.* Charlottesville: University Press of Virginia. Pp. 62–83.

Swamy, P. A. V. B.
    1970. "Efficient Inference in a Random Coefficient Regression Model." *Econometrica* 38 (March): 311–323.

Theil, Henri.
    1954. *Linear Aggregation in Economic Relations.* Amsterdam: North Holland Publishing Company.
    1959. "The Aggregation Implications of Identifiable Structure Macrorelations." *Econometrica* 27 (January): 14–29.
    1960. "Alternative Approaches to the Aggregation Problem." In *Logic, Methodology and the Philosophy of Science.* Edited by E. Nagel, P. Suppes, and A. Tarski. Stanford, Calif.: Stanford University Press. Pp. 507–527.
    1961. *Economic Forecasts and Policy.* Amsterdam: North Holland Publishing Company. (2nd revised ed.)

Thomas, Edwin N., and Anderson, David L.
    1965. "Additional Comments on Weighting Values in Correlation Analysis of Areal Data." *Annals of the Association of American Geographers* 55 (September): 492–505.

Thorndike, Edward L.
    1939. "On the Fallacy of Imputing the Correlations Found for Groups to the Individuals or Smaller Groups Composing Them." *American Journal of Psychology* 52 (January): 122–124.

Tinbergen, Jan.
    1939.   *Statistical Testing of Business Cycle Theories: A Method and Its Application to Investment Activity.* Geneva: League of Nations.

Valkonen, Tapani.
    1969.   "Individual and Structural Effects in Ecological Research." In *Quantitative Ecological Analysis in the Social Sciences.* Edited by M. Dogan and S. Rokkan. Cambridge, Mass.: MIT Press. Pp. 53–68.

Wagner, Helmut R.
    1964.   "Displacement of Scope: A Problem of the Relationship Between Small-Scale and Large-Scale Sociological Theories." *American Journal of Sociology* 69 (May): 571–584.

Wright, Sewall.
    1968.   *Evolution and the Genetics of Populations,* Vol. 1: *Genetic and Biometric Foundations.* Chicago: University of Chicago Press.

Yule, G. Udny, and Kendall, Maurice G.
    1950.   *An Introduction to the Theory of Statistics.* London: Charles Griffin.

Zellner, Arnold.
    1969.   "On the Aggregation Problem: A New Approach to a Troublesome Problem." In *Economic Models, Estimation and Risk Programming.* Edited by K. A. Fox et al. Berlin: Springer-Verlag. Pp. 365–374.

Index

143

About the Author

Michael T. Hannan is currently Assistant Professor of Sociology at Stanford University. He received his Ph.D. from the University of North Carolina at Chapel Hill in 1970. In addition to work on quantitative methodology, he is researching the sociological effects of income maintenance experiments and conducting a cross-national study of educational expansion and economic and political development.